MW01244503

THE ENTREPRENEUR'S PATH

A HANDBOOK
FOR HIGH-GROWTH COMPANIES

ISBN: 978-0-615-43250-2

Why This Handbook?

Back in the heat of the dot.com era, there was a very successful book called *The Monk and the Riddle*. That book told a story about an angel investor helping an entrepreneur with a start-up online funeral supply company. Lenny, the entrepreneur in the story, thought he had the most original idea in the world. His company was going to put the "fun" back in funerals by selling everything from caskets to flowers online.

For me the book had two messages. The first was that it takes enormous personal commitment to start a business and that the only reason to make that kind of commitment is because you have an authentic and deep passion for what you are doing. The second message was that it's nearly impossible to start a business alone. Entrepreneurs need to reach out for advice, mentorship, and guidance as Randy Komisar provides in his book.

I read *The Monk and the Riddle* on an airplane flying across the country on a Friday night. The next Monday I came into the office to meet with a new client, who, like Lenny in the book, began to tell me how unique his business was, and, I kid you not, he was proposing an online funeral company!

I handed him my copy of *The Monk and the Riddle* and said, "You know, before we talk, you really need to read this book."

Not long after that, I was asked to design a university class on new venture startup. We wanted to give the students practical hands-on lessons in what it is like to be entrepreneur building a business plan and raising capital. The first thing we asked each student to do was to create an innovative concept that they thought could change the business world.

We had a room full of bright ideas.

Then we asked the students to value their ideas and prove to themselves and eventually to others that those ideas could actually become profitable businesses someday. That was a bigger challenge for the students, and it helped clarify something for me.

Of the hundreds of entrepreneurs that I've worked with over the years, the ones who were most successful—whether measured by creativity, company growth, profitability, or the size of the exit—all had one thing in common. They followed a path marked by milestones from a good idea to the creation of a successful company. The path isn't smooth or linear. It twists and turns. But there are certain things an entrepreneur just has to know and certain mistakes that he or she cannot afford to make.

This handbook presents that path.

It is not intended as the be-all or end-all of entrepreneurial advice. It is written as a straightforward guide for creative entrepreneurs who have good ideas and want practical and real world advice about the steps they need to follow to increase their chances of turning those good ideas into successful companies.

Keep it with you and refer to it over time. It will help.

Acknowledgements

Writing a book is not a singular exercise. It takes a great many people to assist in researching, collecting, and preparing the material and then in reviewing and editing. And in my case it also takes a translator to convert my engineer-speak to readable sentences.

Thanks to the entire staff at i2E. Your tireless support, dedication and expertise have helped hundreds of entrepreneurs successfully start and grow companies by following the steps along the Entrepreneur's Path. Your collective wisdom and experience is reflected in your contributions to this book.

i2E is a private not-for-profit corporation focused on wealth creation by growing the technology-based entrepreneurial economy in Oklahoma. The public and private sector leaders on our Board of Directors represent business, government, foundations, and academia and share a commitment to strengthening the innovation economy by doing the possible and sometimes the seemingly impossible to expand the entrepreneurial ecosystem. They have our admiration and thanks.

We are able to accomplish our mission in large part through support from the Oklahoma Center for the Advancement of Science and Technology (OCAST). We thank OCAST and the state of Oklahoma for their ongoing financial support.

The success of i2E and our client companies also relies on the contributions of many other individuals and organizations who invest their time, expertise, and capital in Oklahoma's start-up technology companies. There are many excellent resources for entrepreneurs beyond our state who have been generous in sharing best practices. We also appreciate their help.

I would like to thank entrepreneurs for being the reason behind this book. Your creativity, passion, and drive build companies, jobs, and wealth. Without the new businesses and industries that you create, our economy cannot grow.

Special thanks to the marketing and design team of Sarah Seagraves and Jeff Martin for creating a layout for this handbook that is pleasing to look at and easy to follow.

Finally, I would like to thank my "translator" and editor of this book, Mary Jane Grinstead. Mary Jane was a successful technology industry executive in both large companies and startup businesses, who, just like in *The Monk and the Riddle*, followed her passion for writing to start her own business and a second career. She helped us turn our idea for a handbook into *The Entrepreneur's Path*.

Tom D. Walker

Tom D. Walker
President and CEO, i2E, Inc.

Table of Contents

– *Introduction* –

You want to start a high growth business.
We want you to succeed!

We've met thousands of entrepreneurs and helped hundreds of startup companies, and, to borrow a line from Will Rogers, Oklahoma's favorite son, ***"We never met an entrepreneur we didn't like."***

Entrepreneurs are passionate. They make the impossible possible. They don't know the meaning of the word "no." We've learned without a doubt that every entrepreneur and every new business is somehow different from the next.

We've also learned that the path to successfully starting high technology companies is similar whether the business produces the latest electronic gadget, the newest nanotechnology, a green energy solution, or a break-through in life sciences.

The journey begins with an entrepreneur who has passion, persistence, and a good idea that might solve a big problem for a large market. If you are one of those entrepreneurs, this handbook will help you take your best shot at turning your big idea into a viable, sustainable company.

Entrepreneurship is a career field. It brings to mind the saying, "You can lead a horse to water, but you can't saddle a duck." Before you make the leap into entrepreneurship, make sure it's the right pond for you. In other words, if you simply need a job, entrepreneurship may not be the answer.

From planning your business, to attracting risk investment, to telling your story, *The Entrepreneur's Path, A Handbook for High-growth Entrepreneurs* is your go-to guide.

For more than a decade, i2E has been helping entrepreneurs turn their ideas and innovations into successful enterprises. Each year we serve more than 200 entrepreneurs, innovators, and companies representing life sciences, information technology and software, energy, advanced materials, and manufacturing.

The companies in our portfolio are in all stages of business development. Some companies are producing revenues while others are still in pre-revenue stages. Some are led by first-time entrepreneurs; others are founded by serial entrepreneurs who have started companies before.

We work closely with investors, business and community leaders, public sector entities, colleges and universities, and other organizations in the entrepreneurial ecosystem. We are active in the national and international angel investment community.

Together we've learned what does and does not work. We've changed and adapted. We've blended our own best practices with innovative ideas from across the country and around the world.

This handbook represents the full extent of our learned experience. It offers tested and proven tools, templates, and how-to information for entrepreneurs.

Although written for entrepreneurs, *The Entrepreneur's Path* can also be an excellent resource or reference for others who participate in the entrepreneurial ecosystem—investors, government leaders, economic developers, business people, and members of boards of directors.

It can be a supplemental text for educators who are teaching graduate and or undergraduate courses in entrepreneurship. It can help scientists and innovators who don't have prior business experience understand what it takes to turn a technology into a business.

Every entrepreneur has a unique set of skills and experiences. We've added *Tips from the Trenches* as lessons learned from seasoned entrpreneurs.

We've also called on Will Rogers' endearing wit to add a little humor along the way. An independent and self-made man, Will was an original. If he were around, we think he'd find a lot in common with today's entrepreneurs.

Our one-liners may not be as pithy as Will's, but i2E's team of professional advisors, our nationally recognized program of services, and the resources found on our Web site at **www.i2E.org** can add to the customized mix of coaching, tools, and training you will find in this guide.

We encourage you to begin by reading cover to cover. Some sections will be useful immediately; others will be more meaningful to you later on. As you turn your entrepreneurial idea into a business, all the information will eventually become relevant.

Enjoy!

"Even if you're on the right track, you'll get run over if you just sit there."

– *Will Rogers*

THE PATH

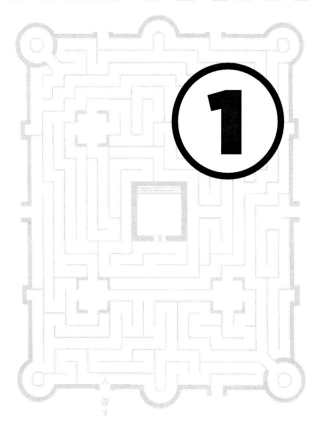

You have an idea. You have passion and determination.
You are ready to turn your idea into a company,
and you know you need some help.

Congratulations!

You've come to the right place. This handbook is written expressly for entrepreneurs who want to create high growth businesses.

High growth businesses are generally founded on state-of-the-art products or processes, and typically have some level of proprietary status. These businesses include:

- **Advanced materials**
- **Aerospace**
- **Agro-sciences**
- **Biosciences**
- **Communications Technologies**
- **Electronics and related fields**
- **Energy**
- **Information Technology**
- **Medical Devices**
- **Medical Instruments**
- **Nanotechnology Robotics**
- **Telecommunications**

... to name a few.

FACTOID

There are 29 million small businesses in the United States according to the Small Business Administration (SBA). Since 2004, yearly averages of 650,000 new companies are launched. It's a pretty likely wager that those businesses began with an idea from an innovator or entrepreneur like you.

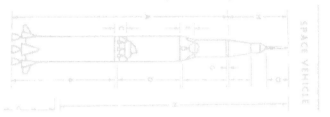

Entrepreneurial ideas may originate in an "aha" moment of inspiration or develop slowly over a period of time. They may involve writing proprietary software or developing applications from open source code.

Sometimes they come from putting together existing components in innovative and unusual ways or from years of laboratory experimentation and bench research that leads to a new discovery, invention, or technology. Other times groundbreaking ideas appear behind the closed eyelids of soon-to-be entrepreneurs while they are lying on the beach.

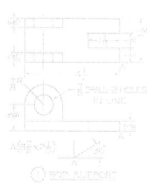

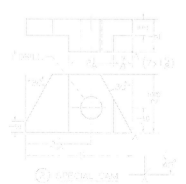

Whenever and however the "aha" moment arrives and the decision is made to turn that idea into a product or service, the **Entrepreneurial Path** begins.

The Entrepreneurial Path

The Entrepreneurial Path *is* the path you will be following as you take your big idea from Proof-of-Concept to Growth.

We will lay out a path of critical milestones required to succeed at each stage to progress to the next. The sequence of milestones and actual events on the path will vary from company to company. Every new company that continues to survive and progress will experience each of these stages, sometimes more than once.

The Entrepreneur's Path focuses on the first five stages of the company's existence; **Proof-of-Concept, Seed, Startup, Early,** and **Growth**. These stages typically span the first three to five years of a company's life.

Proof-of-Concept: The business concept is developed.

Seed: The company has a product or service at a very early stage of development but probably not fully operational.

Startup: The business functions of the company are created; the initial management team is in place. The first prototype is more developed.

Early: Beta testing has begun and company may be approaching breakeven with respect to expense and revenue.

Growth: Company is producing revenue and profitable.

Later Stage to Maturity: Product or service is widely available. Acquisition IPO, or continue to innovate and operate as a private company.

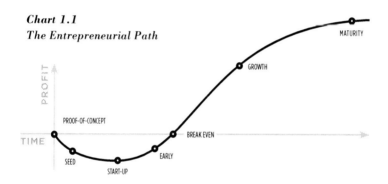

Chart 1.1
The Entrepreneurial Path

As you follow the path of this handbook, you will learn more vocabulary of the entrepreneurial world. Start using the names of these stages to describe your company. Become comfortable using these terms when you talk to investors, service providers, business people and other entrepreneurs.

Using entrepreneurial language helps others understand where you are and demonstrates that you understand, too.

Matching Sources of Capital to the Milestones of the Entrepreneurial Path

All high growth businesses require risk capital. Each stage of the Entrepreneurial Path has a corresponding stage and source of capital. Understanding the stages and sources of capital focuses the management team's efforts. Focusing on the correct capital source and identifying achievable milestones will simplify and improve the success of the capital raising process and focus the management team's efforts.

This seems to be one of the hardest fundamentals for entrepreneurs to learn.

For example, the Proof-of-Concept Stage is no time to be seeking venture capital. We can't count the number of times we've heard entrepreneurs say that **"several venture capitalists are interested in investing,"** when we know that only a very small percentage of all venture capital is directed at companies that are not producing revenue.

FACTOID

The last few years, according to the National Association of Venture Capitalists, only 2 percent of all venture capital went to seed investments and some statistics report that only 1 percent of the businesses targeting venture capital firms for dollars actually receive an investment.

As these statistics shout, except for the biotechnology and life sciences industries, venture capital funding is an unlikely option for an entrepreneurial company until the business is producing revenue. Yes, there are outliers that attract venture capitalists early, but the vast majority of deals do not fall into this category.

Don't jump ahead and try to attract capital from an investor type before your company reaches the stage where that investor likes to invest. That's equivalent to fishing for catfish in a mountain trout stream. It's a waste of your time and theirs.

So how *do* you target the right source of capital at the right stage? Start by understanding what your company will need capital for and how it will be used at each stage of the Entrepreneurial Path to achieve important milestones.

CAPITAL REQUIREMENTS PER STAGE

Proof-of-Concept: Proof-of-concept funding is usually the first capital that a business attempts to access. It is used to incorporate the business, invest in appropriate protections for the technology, and create a limited prototype of the product or service.

Seed: Seed investment rounds typically provide capital to prove the feasibility of the product and quantify the market.

Startup: Startup capital, typically referred to as first round or Series A, and used to fund the introduction of a working product prototype or pilot to the market to verify that the economics of the business plan are sustainable. With shifting financial markets, this round is often an extension of the seed round.

Early: These equity rounds that occur after the seed and startup rounds, commonly referred to as first or second round or Series B and so on, are typically used to fund product and market development. Early Stage is often referred to as the stage when a company is generating revenue based on its business model.

Growth: This equity capital is used to fund expansion and growth. Depending on the business, certain types of bank loans may be applicable.

Later Stage to Maturity: Equity capital and traditional funds support expansion, growth, and potentially strategic acquisitions to enter new markets.

There is one more term that entrepreneurs will hear during discussions of capital requirements – The Valley of Death. This is the point during the Proof-of-Concept, Seed, Startup, and Early Stage when the company is spending more money that it is taking in, usually to build product and carry out market development. It is called that Valley of Death because so many companies don't make it out of this stage.

Chart 1.2
Matching Capital Sources to the Entrepreneurial Path

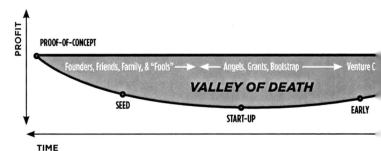

SOURCES OF CAPITAL

Successful entrepreneurs match their company's capital needs with the most appropriate and likely capital source at each stage.

Founders, Friends, Family, and "Fools": You will be your first investor. After that, family, friends, and acquaintances will often invest very early in the company's Path as their trust and interest is in the individual more than monetary returns. You will often hear this group "fondly" referred to as "fools" because this stage of a company's growth is so risky and unpredictable.

Banks: Local banks, and to some extent national ones, may be a source of lines of credit, traditional borrowing, or convertible debt. The more personal resources the founder and/or company has, the more possible this source is.

Grants: Business grants come from public and private sector, not-for-profit foundations and other entities. Typically, grants are used in the early research and development stage of a company to further the technology. Unlike loans, grants do not have to be repaid. Grants, like equity capital, are time intensive to attract and the entrepreneur must be targeted in his or her approach.

Bootstrap: Bootstrapping requires entrepreneurs to use imagination, know-how, and hard work to pay as they go through revenue without raising equity capital. These make the most interesting companies and entrepreneurs.

Angel Investor: Private, high net worth individuals who meet the criteria of accredited investor and invest their own capital in seed and early stage businesses.

Venture Capital: Institutional investors with a typical investment threshold of at least $2 million in exchange for equity in early and later stage businesses.

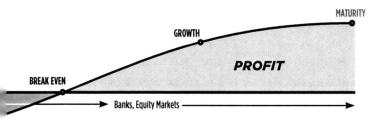

MAKING YOUR BIG IDEA REAL

You bring the idea. *The Entrepreneur's Path* provides the framework, tools, and process to validate the business potential of your entrepreneurial dream.

This chapter has introduced you to the Entrepreneur's Path and the Sources and Uses of Capital. In the following chapters, we provide tools, processes, thought-starters, and information on best practices. These will help entrepreneurs reduce the risk that is inherent in new companies and achieve the critical milestones along the path from Proof-of-Concept to Growth Stage.

1. THE RISK – Entrepreneur's Risk Assessment: This is a thought-starter for evaluating the activities that relate to the **product or service** you plan to provide, the **market** your product will serve, and the viability of the **business** you want to build. The general risk for the aspects of *product*, *market*, *business*, *finance*, and *execution* will be addressed in your business plan.

2. THE CASH – Capital Sources: Get real about the fine art of raising capital. Learn about the money that may be available to entrepreneurs and how to increase your chances of getting some of it. Understand the importance of the Entrepreneurial Path as it pertains to capital requirements and sources for your company. Learn how to develop informed tactical and strategic plans to reach a realistic and achievable capital plan to move your company through the Path and over time to long-term sustainability.

3. THE PLAN – Business Plan Checklist: The business plan checklist provides an overview of key philosophies related to writing a business plan, questions the plan must answer, and statements and misconceptions to avoid.

4. THE PITCH
Elevator Speech: Learn the "hows" and "whys" of developing the perfect elevator speech that describes your business and its opportunity for the market and investors in less than fifty words.

Business Plan Pitch: The handbook provides guidelines on content, approach, and a presentation template to help entrepreneurs deliver a business plan pitch that earns investors' attention.

5. THE PRICE – Valuation Model and Sample Term Sheets: Learn how to approach valuation from an investor's viewpoint to attract capital and create a collaborative relationship with the people who control the purse.

6. THE RELATIONSHIPS – Relationship Building: We offer examples of techniques and best practices in productive networking, establishing an advisory board, and creating an effective board of directors that will help your company grow.

7. THE EXIT – Exit Strategies: In the beginning, you may be so consumed with product and market strategies that it seems impossible to invest any energy in considering the milestones of the later stages of company growth, but exits are always on investors' minds. Learn the basics of investor exit strategies–good and bad–including fire sale, initial public offerings (IPO), and acquisition.

CONCLUSION

Whether your idea is still just a dream or already has an address, there is no one-size-fits-all, turnkey approach to starting your company. The first thirty days of any new venture will prove that.

On the other hand, many of the same issues and risks are present in almost all advanced technology start-ups. While this handbook does not supply all the answers, it helps you ask the right questions, at the right time, of the right folks.

Key Points

While each entrepreneur and company is unique; the stages and milestones of the Entrepreneurial Path are common to all.

Successful entrepreneurs match their company's capital needs with the most appropriate and likely to invest capital source at each stage of the Entrepreneurial Path.

You bring the idea. *The Entrepreneur's Path* provides the framework, tools, and process to validate the business potential of your entrepreneurial dream.

"You've got to go out on a limb sometimes because that's where the fruit is."

– Will Rogers

THE RISK

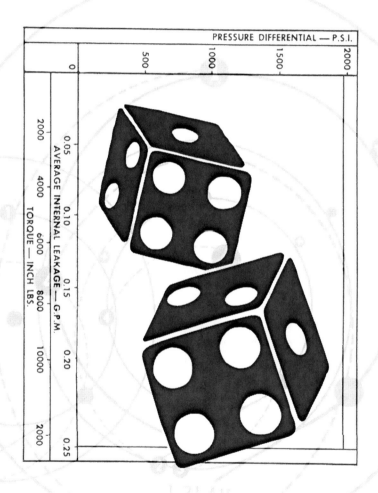

2

Since the IPO boom of the late nineties through more challenging recent times, we have interacted with more than 2,000 high growth companies which span the spectrum of advanced technology businesses.

Many of the companies we met became our clients and are following our disciplined approach to turn their ideas into products and services that customers buy. Are they all going to succeed? Probably not. Starting a new company is a very risky business.

FACTOID

Since 2004, a yearly average of 575,000 small businesses (about 20 percent) ceased operations. Three in ten new firms don't make it past 24 months, and about half of the ones that do, don't survive more than five years, according to Business Dynamics Statistics compiled by the U.S. Census Bureau.

On the other hand, for every three new companies that don't make it through twenty-four months, seven others survive. And while about half of those seven fail in the next five years, the other half of them don't. They continue, creating jobs, revenue, and breakthrough innovations. That is the funnel of startup innovation. Out of ten great ideas, two to three make it.

BUILDING A PRODUCT AND BUILDING A BUSINESS ARE NOT THE SAME THING

Entrepreneurs are passionate about their technologies. In the beginning, the company, the product or service, and the technology are so closely related that it's hard to think about them independently.

From the start, innovators and entrepreneurs have to focus most of their energy and resources on developing their product. There is a tendency to give lip service, postpone, or totally ignore any analysis of the market they are hoping to serve and whether that market is substantial enough to support the new company.

"If you build it they will come" may work for the Field of Dreams or Trump Tower, but never, no not even once, in all our years of working with entrepreneurs have we seen this strategy work for a start-up company, no matter how innovative or amazing the technology, product, or service was.

The cold hard truth of high growth entrepreneurship is that unless you deliver a product or service that thousands and thousands of people want to buy and can pay for, your company will likely be one of the seven in ten that don't succeed.

"Before you move very far or very fast in the direction of taking your idea, product, or service from concept to market, take the time to invest a portion of your scarce resources—including your passion, creativity, energy, money, and time—to finding out everything you possibly can about the market and customers you want to serve."

WHAT PROBLEM ARE YOU SOLVING AND FOR WHOM?

As an entrepreneur on the path to success, you must be able to articulate the market problem you are trying to solve. Prove to yourself and others that there is reasonable basis for believing that the people and companies in the market you plan to serve will pay your company for your solution to the problem they have.

It isn't to say that your product or service can't be the secret sauce in your company's success. Many times it is, but always, always view products and technologies in the context of the marketplace and the needs of potential customers.

As you think about your big idea, paraphrasing the words of entrepreneur and author, Guy Kawasaki in his book *The art of the start*, "What's the big problem, and what's your big solution?" Is the market clamoring for a solution that your product and service solves? Is this market large enough to create a business?

Another way to look at this issue is as follows: You have a product that solves a problem in the market. How large *is* the market? Is the product/market combination large enough to merit forming a company? Remember, a product does not make a company.

Let's assume that you've performed the analysis and legwork to show how your company's products and services can solve big problems in a large market. What's next? What steps do you take to make your business be one of the seven in ten that gets through the first 24 months and goes on to survive five years or more? How do you find the potholes ahead of time?

THE ENTREPRENEUR'S RISK ASSESSMENT

To say that entrepreneurial businesses are risky is kind of like saying the sky is blue. From day one, every new company faces risks.

High growth start-ups that gain traction, attract equity capital and great employees, and win the confidence of early adopters do so because they have determined where the risks are at every stage along the Entrepreneurial Path and have developed tactical and strategic plans to maneuver through.

Your company will face five areas of risk: product, market, business, finance, and execution.

Product: A tangible object, technology, or service offered for sale.

Market: A commercial activity where goods and services are sold.

Business: A commercial enterprise that produces a product or service to be sold to a market.

Finance: The capital and cash flow required to achieve milestones that lead to success.

Execution: The experience, skills, and processes required to carry out a business plan.

It's also a given that predictions are imperfect and that there will be plenty of surprises and mistakes along the way, but if you start out anticipating that these will occur and conduct scenario planning in case they do, you will greatly enhance your chances of success.

The point is, if you want to attract investors' attention, anticipate and quantify risks and allow for the inevitability of unexpected events in your business plan and business pitch.

 Many entrepreneurs are used to being subject matter experts–especially if they are in a technology field. Instead of trying to show everyone what you do know, be coachable. Ask questions and listen to find out what you don't know. It may be a much longer conversation than you expect.

THE ENTREPRENEUR'S RISK ASSESSMENT PROCESS

The **Entrepreneur's Risk Assessment** is a thought process which guides you through developing a mental foundation for your company's business plan and capital strategy.

The following is not intended to be a cookbook for risk assessment, but rather a thought starter to help you think like an investor in your business, which in a very real way you are.

Keep in mind the path that we outlined in Chapter 1 as you read this chapter and refer back to **Chart 1.2**.

PROOF-OF-CONCEPT STAGE RISK

Risk Profile: At the Proof-of-Concept Stage, you have a new product or technology that seems to have market potential. You have limited financial resources and, unless you have founded a company before, your expertise in taking a product or service from concept to market is probably limited.

The **product risk** is that the product or service may not be feasible, may lack unique qualities that cannot be adequately protected, or may be too difficult or expensive to produce in quantity.

The **market risk** is that the entrepreneur has limited understanding or knowledge of the market and overstates the size or growth potential.

The **business risk** is that a great product or technology doesn't always translate into a great business.

The **finance risk** is that funding for Proof-of-Concept is hard to find.

The **execution risk** is that the innovator or entrepreneur may lack business skills.

You gather evidence to prove (or disprove) that your technology or product is viable and capable of solving a particular problem for a particular market. You have developed an initial business plan and invested weeks and months of your own time, some of your own money, and maybe even resources from family and friends.

It's time to make the call. Is your business a go, or no go? If it's a go, you are ready to consider Seed Stage risk.

SEED STAGE RISK

Risk Profile: The final design of the product or service is complete and your initial business plan is in place. The company's management team is incomplete. With no product revenues, the company is burning through cash and other resources.

The **product risk** is that the company is focused on product innovation rather than business development. Intellectual property rights remain a concern.

The **market risk** is that unrealistic market study results cause misallocation of scarce resources.

The **business risk** is the company lacks depth in business formation and commercialization.

The **finance risk** is that cash flow is a problem and Seed Stage funding is difficult to find and attract.

The **execution risk** is that the management team is incomplete and stretched thin. Investors are looking for experienced teams, but the company can't hire that experience until it receives funding.

As the company moves from Seed to Startup Stage, development of the product prototype continues.

STARTUP STAGE RISK

Risk Profile: The company continues to develop the product prototype, working toward specified milestone completion dates. Significant expenses are incurred with no product-related revenues. Companies that progress to the Startup Stage, usually experience their riskiest pre-revenue point in the "Valley of Death."

The **product risk** is that as the product or service advances from development into production, new skills are needed.

The **market risk** is that field tests with customers are not positive or that competitors respond more rapidly than expected.

The **business risk** is that as decisions for strategic partnerships, licensing agreements, and channel strategies are needed, the founding management team may lack professional experience.

The **finance risk** is that significant expenses occur without produce revenue being realized.

The **execution risk** is that the founders and management team lose focus or resist implementing appropriate business controls. The founder or members of the early team may exit the business.

As business development moves into sales, the company builds marketing and customer relationships that position it for the moving the product into the market place to gain acceptance from paying customers.

EARLY STAGE RISK

Risk Profile: The company has limited product revenues as the product enters the market place.

The **product risk** is that product features reveal a limited market-driven functionality after scaling up product.

The **market risk** is that the reality of the market is rarely as planned. Lower market acceptance, aggressive competition, and limited repeat business can affect revenue.

The **business risk** is that the company can't make the transition from a Seed to Startup environment to a true mode of business operation.

The **finance risk** is that the burn rate exceeds capital and management focuses on sales instead of profits.

The **execution risk** is that founding management and employees cannot keep up with the accelerating pace of change and have difficulty adapting to new business strategies.

As products become established in the marketplace, physical distribution is finalized and required production facilities are contracted or built. The company initiates quality control and processes.

GROWTH STAGE RISK

Risk Profile: The company is in full production with the main product and is expanding distribution. Customers are paying for product or service. Management is in transition to a formal organization structure.

The **product risk** is that product features must be refined to stay competitive. The demand for new features drains human and financial resources.

The **market risk** is that there are problems with distribution, customer satisfaction, or features. Competitors respond to product launch.

The **business risk** is that focus and business skills become more of an issue as operational demands increase.

The **finance risk** is that poor strategies of resource allocation limit the ability to increase expertise through training or hiring and impact ability to execute new contracts with customers.

The **execution risk** is that the startup buzz is gone. Hiring new people and increased focus on roles causes employees to become more focused on their functional responsibilities and less focused on the overall company mission. The entrepreneurial culture can change.

As the company becomes more well-established in the marketplace, management must continually innovate to stay competitive.

LATER STAGE TO MATURITY RISK

Risk Profile: The ability to innovate in all areas – product, market, business, finance, and execution is vital to the firm's long-term sustainability and growth.

The **product risk** is that volume declines as products mature.

The **market risk** is that the entrepreneur has limited understanding or knowledge of the market and overstates the size or growth potential.

The **business risk** is that the pressures of monthly and quarterly financial goals limit the ability and resources to innovate.

The **finance risk** is that poor strategies of resource allocation limit the ability to increase expertise through training or hiring and impact ability to execute new contracts with customers.

The **execution risk** is that a structured corporate environment makes it difficult to innovate.

In real life, companies are not built in a straightforward fashion. Every entrepreneurial situation is unique. For your company, the risks we've summarized in this chapter may occur "out of order." But rest assured they will occur.

GUIDING PRINCIPLES OF ASSESSING AND MANAGING RISK

Even though one of the best things about entrepreneurship is that there are no hard and fast rules, these principles will increase your efficiency and improve your company's odds of survival.

- Become a student of the Entrepreneurial Path.
- Anticipate addressing the product, market, and business activities and risks of each stage before moving to the next stage on the path.
- Be credible and avoid common misconceptions of the entrepreneurial process.
- Learn everything possible about the customer.
- Achieve market validation as soon as possible – this means sales.
- Develop a profitable business model.
- Success depends on profit; profit depends on growth.
- Growth depends on sales; sales depend on new innovations.
- Don't count on partners to do your selling for you.
- Accept that raising a significant amount of capital initially is not necessary or even desirable.

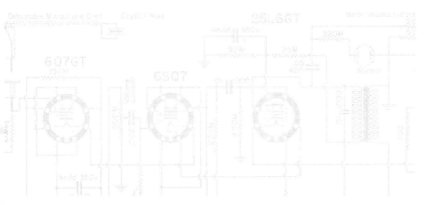

CONCLUSION

When you are founding a company, preparing mentally for unwelcome or unexpected events helps you anticipate situations so that when you find your company in the heat of the battle, you have a head start on a game plan to tackle and conquer the risks.

This mental toughness positions you and your business to be among the 50 percent of new companies that survive five years or more.

KEY POINTS

Building a product and building a business are not the same thing.

Successful companies turn their product or service into problem solving solutions for big markets.

All new companies face risks. It's up to you as founder to understand the risks at every stage on the path and then to develop tactical and strategic plans to maneuver your way through.

Expect surprises every day.

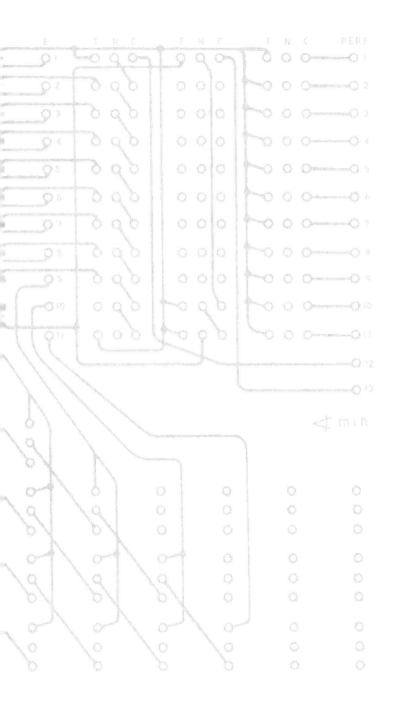

"Get someone else to blow your horn and the sound will carry twice as far."

– *Will Rogers*

THE CASH

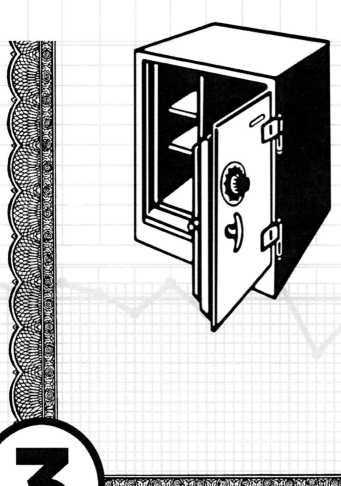

3

The Entrepreneurial Path is measured in terms of the time it takes to achieve a certain level of profitability. Profit allows a business to cover expenses, pay investors, repay debts, reward key contributors, and invest to achieve future growth or attract a buyer if acquisition is the goal. The sooner a company reaches profitability the better.

Starting out, most companies are not profitable. In fact, many startups go through a period of significant capital losses or negative profitability. Until the company can raise money through revenue, it must find other sources of capital. Outside investment is achieved by targeting the right sources of capital at the right stage of business growth.

One of the most common misconceptions by entrepreneurs is that they must raise a great deal of capital up front to succeed. This is simply not true. There are many, many entrepreneurs—especially in the years before and after the dotcom bubble—who started with very little capital investment.

Companies such as Cisco, Oracle, Microsoft, Mary Kay Cosmetics, and UPS are modern era business success stories that started with relatively modest amounts of up-front investment.

Stanford professors Leonard Bosack and Sandy Lerner had a need to e-mail each other but could not because each had non-compatible systems. After achieving proof-of-concept, they developed a router to accomplish their need. This husband and wife team went on to start Cisco in 1984 to commercialize their innovation. Funded through credit cards and revenue growth, Cisco was profitable with over $2.5 million in annual revenue before receiving venture capital from Sequoia Capital in 1987. Turns out, they never spent it!

There are plenty of other companies that started with less than $10,000: Apple Computer, Dell Computer, Gateway, Papa John's Pizza, and Ernst and Julio Gallo, to name only a few.

This isn't to minimize an entrepreneur's need to focus on capital. It just emphasizes that there are lots of ways for creative and focused entrepreneurs to move their ideas along the path from bright idea to prototype without having to raise bundles of capital.

And that's a good thing, because raising large amounts of capital in the beginning stages of the Entrepreneurial Path is very difficult and can consume far too much of the entrepreneur's time.

DEVELOPING A CAPITAL PLAN

Founders, Friends, and Family
Customers/Strategic ~ Banks ~ Grants ~ Bootstrap
Angel Investment ~Venture Capital ~ IPO

Developing a capital strategy and plan based on focusing on the correct capital source and identifying achievable milestones that follow the flow of the Entrepreneurial Path can simplify the capital raising process.

Take a moment to review the chart in Chapter 1.

Chart 3.1
The Capital Path

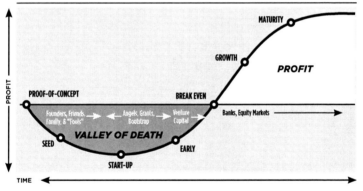

Traversing the capital path is not usually accomplished in such a straightforward fashion as is presented in this graph. The principles are the same for each business, but from one company to the next the experience is different.

Some companies may accelerate through certain stages; other companies may move forward and then step backward before they move forward again. And still other companies falter before they can raise or earn enough capital to succeed.

CAPITAL MARKET-SPEAK

To move along the path of developing an investment strategy, you first have to learn and understand the language of the capital markets.

Angel investor: An angel investor is a wealthy individual who provides capital for a startup business in return for ownership shares in the business or convertible debt. Angels often organize into angel groups or angel networks to share deal flow, due diligence on potential investment companies, and to pool their investment capital.

Convertible debt: Some investors and banks will offer capital under terms of convertible debt. In these borrowing arrangements, the lender has the option to convert the debt into shares of equity at a specified point in time.

Dry powder: Savvy investors often hold back a portion of investment capital in anticipation of unexpected events.

Equity Investment: Investments made in return for a percentage ownership in the company, which usually takes the form of common or preferred shares of stock.

First Round, Second Round: This ordinal nomenclature is used to describe most venture rounds. Companies will casually call their rounds first, second, third, etc. even though the legal term for the transaction as stated in closing documents and amendments to the documents of incorporation may refer to them as Series A preferred, Series B common, etc.

Grants: Grants come from businesses, foundations, and public and private sector organizations. Some grants require the entrepreneur to come up with matching funds from other sources. Unlike loans or equity capital from investors, grants do not have to be repaid.

Initial Public Offering: IPO stands for initial public offering and occurs when a company first sells shares of its stock to the public.

Mezzanine: A mezzanine equity investment round is generally characterized as the last venture round prior to an IPO or some other positive exit event.

Portfolio: Collection of investments made by angels or venture capitalists.

Syndication: Multiple investors, which may include individual angels, angel groups, and venture capitalists, pool their funds to provide larger investments and to diversify risk.

Third, Fourth, Fifth, etc. and Later Rounds: Equity rounds that fall after the second round of financing.

Valuation: Valuation reflects the value of the company before and after the investment of additional equity capital. Establishing the value of a pre-revenue company is challenging and can be an impediment to entrepreneurs raising capital.

Venture Capital: Venture Capital is pooled investment capital from institutional investors and high net worth individuals. Because of the size of VC funds and operating costs, most VC funds find it more efficient to invest $2 million or more. This means they are more likely to seek out high growth technology businesses that are producing revenue with the exception of life sciences.

The investor drives the capital raising process. Always. The entrepreneur must identify and implement realistic milestones to attract investors at each stage of the Entrepreneurial Path.

STAGES OF CAPITAL

We are now ready to discuss in more detail the source of capital that are associated with each stage of the Entrepreneurial Path.

Proof-of-Concept Stage: Founders, Friends, Family, and "Fools"

There is an old saying among seasoned entrepreneurs: "Starting a business usually takes twice as long and costs twice as much as you think it will." It often makes sense to keep your day job and pursue your entrepreneurial ideas after hours in the beginning. Before you take out a home equity loan, max out your credit cards, or tap into your 401(k), achieve some positive progress toward the Proof-of-Concept Stage.

Recognize that sooner or later, if you decide to keep going, you are going to have to take personal financial risk. Anticipate needing between $25,000 and $100,000 to carry your business idea through the Proof-of-Concept Stage. Several million dollars will be needed if the company is in the life sciences industries.

Financing for the Proof-of-Concept Stage primarily comes from the founder's **personal resources** and sometimes from **friends, family, and so-called "fools."** Family, friends, and acquaintances will often invest very early in the company's life as their trust and interest is in the individual than in the possibility of significant monetary returns.

Many entrepreneurs approach friends and family members (in some entrepreneurial circles known as the "Three Fs"– friends, family, and fools). People who know, trust, and like you may be more willing to invest, may accept a lower return on their investment with less collateral (possibly none) than a bank, and may be less likely to examine every detail of your business plan.

That's all well and good. Just be aware that raising money from people you know may also create personal and emotional issues that add to the already heavy stress of founding a business. This isn't to say you shouldn't go this route. Just apply the same good business practices and arms-length relationship to this financial arrangement as you would to any other.

Generally, you will want to have an attorney prepare the appropriate legal documents. Consider structuring friends and family money as debt (with an at-market interest rate) instead of equity. Debt holders can't tell you how to run your business like equity partners can.

Pay off the debt as quickly as you can. Most angel investors and venture capitalists do not want their deals burdened with commitments from earlier rounds. Due to this and depending on the amount of capital needed at this stage, often times a convertible debt to equity instrument is constructed.

 Sometimes entrepreneurs raise friends and family money in exchange for shares of the company. Angel investors are far less likely to invest if they have to deal with lots of small shareholders from prior friends and family rounds. Venture capitalists are even more opposed to it. Be smart and discriminating when attracting capital.

Seed Stage: Founder, Friends and Family, Grants, Banks, and Angel Investors

Once the feasibility of the product or service is reasonably proven, entrepreneurs need additional outside capital to take their idea from concept to a product or service that someone will buy.

Whether economic times are flush or challenging, your goal as an entrepreneur progress from Proof-of-Concept into Seed Stage must be to find creative ways to move your business forward while making 18 months of cash last for 24.

From Proof-of-Concept through Seed Stage, expenses accelerate. The company is in product development mode, and there are no revenues. There is a reason that seasoned entrepreneurs and startup investors sometimes call this stage "the Valley of Death."

Grants: SBIR and STTR Awards

The federal government's **Small Business Innovation Research (SBIR)** and **Small Business Technology Transfer (STTR)** programs can be excellent sources of early capital if the Seed Stage company meets the criteria of the award.

The government provides grants to supplement the limited research and development funding that is available to companies from the private sector.

Additionally, many federal agencies, particularly the Department of Defense, are looking for technologies and products that meet government needs and have commercial applications. Agency SBIR and STTR programs have provided critical, early capital to numerous entrepreneurs.

All federal agencies with an extramural research and development budget of more than $100 million (SBIR) or $1 billion (STTR) must participate in these programs, making them the largest source of early research and development funding for small businesses in the US. Eleven departments participate in the SBIR program and five departments participate in the STTR program. Together they award more than $2 billion to small high-tech businesses annually.

SBIR and STTR grants are very competitive. Still, every advanced technology entrepreneur should know enough about these programs to determine whether or not the company should consider federal grants. When a company's objectives and capabilities match the requirements of the granting agency, these funds can provide significant off-balance sheet funding.

Scientists and inventors from research and development or university backgrounds who are familiar with grant applications and reporting find SBIRs and STTRs a good option. Entrepreneurs who are founding companies to invent a drug or commercialize a nanotechnology application may also identify seeking SBIR or STTR grants as a Seed stage priority.

The grants, which provide financial assistance to companies to execute a certain scope of work, can vary from agency to agency. They cover a range of activities including research and development, testing, evaluation, demonstration, and may even include full-scale commercialization. The scope of work can be tightly or somewhat loosely defined. The company receiving the grant does not guarantee an outcome.

Generally Phase I grants award between $100,000 and $150,000 for activities of about a year or less in duration. Phase II grants are up to $750,000 for typically up to two years. Phase III projects encompass non-SBIR/STTR funding and derive from, extend, or logically conclude efforts performed under prior SBIR contracts.

The recipients of SBIR/STTR grants are required to report progress against the scope of work with a final report at the end of the grant. As long as effort is applied in good faith, there isn't the requirement to meet certain objectives. There is no requirement for the company to return the grant money if project objectives are not achieved.

SBIRs and STTRs are not appropriate for every company. It can be time consuming, especially for a startup company with limited human resources, to apply for an SBIR or STTR grant. It is not a good idea for an entrepreneur to count on a federal grant as the make-or-break funding for Seed Stage activities–especially if that entrepreneur has no prior experience applying for federal grants. The lengthy lead time for grant approval can also be a significant issue for entrepreneurs who need capital in a certain timeframe.

Federal agencies are always looking for advances in technology; they aren't looking for incremental improvements. They want groundbreaking leaps that are faster, less costly, and better than alternatives–and there are always alternatives.

In addition to SBIRs and STTRs, there are other requests for proposals (sometimes called solicitations or RFPs) and agency announcements that may be for a specific technology or encompass multiple technologies and may be for a specific time frame or open to response for years.

These opportunities are posted online by the requesting agency. Savvy entrepreneurs use the Internet to figure out which government agencies and departments might be interested in their solution or technology. It is possible to develop relationships with the program managers who follow technologies like yours. Their areas of interest and requirements are public information.

If you determine that you want to reply to an open SBIR or STTR grant or for some other government request for proposal, you may want to consider seeking the advice and assistance of someone who has been successful at the process previously. This could be another entrepreneur, a trusted mentor in a university or research institution, or a professional grant consultant. Once a company has obtained one grant with an agency, there is often the opportunity to pursue more opportunities.

When an entrepreneur learns how to develop an effective grant proposal for the federal government, that knowledge is applicable to other types of grants.

Bank Lines of Credit and Convertible Notes
Local **banks,** and to some extent national ones, may be a source of lines of credit and traditional debt. Some institutions and angel investors employ convertible notes, which are loans that are convertible to equity at the option of the lender or when certain events occur, such as a subsequent investment round.

As with any loans made to a Seed Stage company, expect a convertible note to carry an above-market interest rate in consideration of your company's risk. Depending on the terms of the loan or convertible notes, if a company lacks the cash flow to make periodic payments, there may be provisions for the interest to accrue for a period of time or until the next funding event.

Angel Investors

Angel investors are **accredited investors** (think high net worth individuals who are millionaires plus) who put their own money and time into companies that are at the seed stage and beyond.

Angels invest in Seed, Startup, and Early Stage opportunities. Their and any equity investor's approach at this stage is to provide a nominal amount of capital to see how the company progresses.

A challenge for entrepreneurs is that even though angel investors do provide about 90 percent of the outside equity that funds the initial stages of entrepreneurial businesses, individual angel investors are almost impossible for entrepreneurs to identify and reach. Angels tend to protect their privacy.

The Angel Capital Association (ACA), the trade organization of North American angel investors posts a member group directory (www. angelcapitalassociation.com). Some angel groups have websites that define their investment strategy and offer a process for business plan submission.

The Angel Capital Association (ACA) is a professional alliance of more than 165 organized angel group members representing about 7,000 accredited investors. These angel groups fund hundreds of companies a year and have an ongoing portfolio of 5,000 companies across the US and Canada.

ACA member groups report averaging about six investments per year in between three and four companies, averaging about $200,000 per investment round.

If as an entrepreneur, you think of angel investors as flinty-eyed wealthy individuals who are out to "steal" your company, readjust your thinking. Besides being about the only source of Seed and Startup Stage capital around, angel investors know how to help coachable entrepreneurs succeed. Remember, many angels became wealthy by being successful entrepreneurs themselves.

Angels are investing to make a high rate of return given the riskiness of the investments they make. Return on investment is the primary measure of their success but not the only reason that angels invest. Many angel investors made their money as entrepreneurs. They enjoy the challenge and the risk of the entrepreneurial environment and like mentoring and advising entrepreneurs. Many angels also are motivated to give back to their communities by helping promising new companies start up.

Angels invest independently, alongside other investors, or as members of organized angel groups. Organized angel groups have proliferated since the late 1990s; there are now groups in almost every state. They serve as a catalyst for Seed and Startup Stage investing.

Angels and angel groups are as unique and different as are entrepreneurs and startup companies. But whether from Silicon Valley or Oklahoma, angel investors are almost always looking for the same thing–a passionate entrepreneur with an idea that solves a big problem for a big market and a five to 30X return on their investment within three to five years, depending on the company's stage of growth and its prior capital investments.

With so little venture capital money being invested in pre-revenue businesses, entrepreneurs need angel investors more today than ever before–for their money, their contacts, their expertise and experience, and their mentoring. That's why it is very important for every entrepreneur to understand what motivates angels, how they like to receive information, what information they want to receive, and how to work with them effectively.

Some angel groups are organized as networks, which each member makes individual decisions on potential investments. Other groups are organized as funds which operate similar to other investment funds.

SeedStep Angels is an Oklahoma angel group of accredited angel investors that provide capital, strategic advice, and mentoring to emerging growth companies to help them achieve market leadership. Typical investments range from $50,000 to $500,000 as a group with individuals having options for side-by-side investments.

Regardless of their investment model, angels usually invest fairly close to home. They are involved with their portfolio companies and prefer to be within a two or three hour drive of their investments. Group members determine the industries where they want to invest. Life sciences, medical devices, information technology, and software are the industries that interest many angel groups.

Angels like to co-invest with other angels, angel groups, and sometimes with venture capitalists. These syndicated rounds offer efficiencies for both the investors and entrepreneurs. It is common for one group of the investors to take the lead, structure the deal terms; perform due diligence, and handle the closing.

Syndication creates larger investment rounds than any single angel or group would raise. Investors benefit from additional quality deal flow and from having extra hands, eyes, and expertise for due diligence. Additional investors provide additional validation of a good investment opportunity. Larger rounds also allow angels to keep some dry powder for unanticipated events.

For the entrepreneur, syndicated rounds may mean that less time is required to raise more money. Raising capital takes the entrepreneur away from building a product and gaining customers. It is to everyone's advantage, especially the entrepreneur, to hold this process to a minimum.

Interestingly, Angel Capital Association members report that in about 60 percent of their deals, they co-invest with venture capitalists.

The ACA directory is a good place to begin the search for angel investors in your geography, but the best way to make contact with angel investors is through referrals.

Startup Stage: Grants, Angel Investors, Bootstrapping

At the Startup Stage it will be important to prioritize the business strategies that best fit the most appropriate financing stage and source. The company is continuing to develop the product prototype incurring significant expense with no product related revenues. The company is usually at the deepest point in the "Valley of Death" at this stage. Business strategies could include licensing, strategic alliances or partnerships, or the pursuit of a business venture.

The Start up requires sufficient startup capital to initiate business operations. The prototype provides the basis for final analysis of technical feasibility, cost, and market acceptance.

Bootstrapping

Bootstrapping–paying as you go with revenue instead of debt or equity capital–stretches your company's resources

– both financial and otherwise – to fund your Seed Stage growth. Bootstrapping can be one of the most cost effective ways to hasten your company's positive cash flow, reducing the business's requirement for equity capital or debt.

From day one, make effective cash management a priority. The survival of your young company is determined as much by the way you prioritize the use of scarce resources–and nothing is more scarce than cash at this point except perhaps your hours of sleep–as it is by the products you create.

Hold fixed costs to a minimum:
- *Share office services and equipment.*
- *Co-locate with another company or move to a business incubator.*
- *Use the computers and servers you have.*
- *Delay capital purchases.*
- *Lease instead of purchase.*
- *Negotiate fees and terms with all service providers*

Treat variable costs like you are spending your own money–which you are:
- *Seek trade credit terms with key suppliers.*
- *Save thousands on travel by smart scheduling and use of the Internet, or don't travel at all.*
- *Speak to your local business school about internships.*

And by the way, these tips for bootstrapping are excellent habits to practice whether you are bootstrapping or not.

Early Stage: Venture Capital

These days, venture capitalists are institutional investors with a typical investment threshold of at least $2 million in exchange for equity in early and later stage businesses. Their economic model usually does not support investment in pre-revenue stage companies. VCs look for entrepreneurs who have a track record of startup success.

In your region, it is common to find smaller venture capital funds of around $5 to $20 million. Funds in this range, may make smaller investments. However, their investment process and investment terms are similar to larger VC funds.

Similar to angels, venture capitalists seek a return potential of over ten times their investment in about five years. Like angel investors, VCs like to syndicate. However, there are also venture capital funds that do not syndicate.

To create enough upside opportunity to justify their effort and resources, VCs need to invest $3 to $5 million or more per deal. This means that VCs usually look for companies that are further along the growth curve and generating revenues from customer sales. Venture capitalists will want to speak with existing customers as part of their due diligence.

Growth Stage through Maturity: Initial Public Offering

The first sale of your stock as a private company to the public is called an Initial Public Offering (IPO).

An IPO raises cash and creates other benefits for the company. A public company can always issue more stock, although there is no guarantee there will be buyers. If there are, those shares will raise more cash.

Going public requires the company to strictly conform to rules of the Securities and Exchange Commission (SEC), which extensive financial reporting, the creation of a board of directors, and other regulations.

We cannot over-emphasize that IPOs are few and far between. That's why we don't invest much time on them. If you want more information on IPOs, use the Internet. Keep in mind, less than 20% of all venture-backed companies have IPOs.

Manage cash

No matter how successful you are at raising capital, sooner or later, your new company will be cash strapped. Regardless of your stage of entrepreneurial development, become really smart about managing cash. If capital is required, do not delay.

- *Consider bootstrapping or friends and family first.*
- *Build a relationship with local banks.*
- *Micro-lenders will loan from $5,000 to $50,000.*
- *Be prepared to provide extensive information to prove credit-worthiness.*
- *Stay alert for federal or state tax credits or stimulus incentives for startup or high technology businesses.*

CONCLUSION

Every entrepreneur eventually will need to raise capital to fund the milestones that lead to sustainable revenue. The process starts with understanding those milestones, then understanding the appropriate sources of capital, and then matching up the two in a well-formed business plan.

If you have a day job, keep it until you are certain your entrepreneurial idea can gain enough traction to become cash flow positive. Seek out experienced business people and entrepreneurs for advice and mentoring. Don't allow optimism and passion to override practicality.

Carve out some time every week to de-compress. A rock-sure way for a company to fail is to have the founder suffer a heart attack.

KEY POINTS

The Entrepreneurial Lifecycle is measured in terms of the time it takes to achieve a certain level of profitability.

Until the company can raise money through revenue, it must find other sources of capital.

To move along the path of developing an investment strategy, you have to understand the language of the capital markets.

One of the most common misconceptions by entrepreneurs is that they must raise a great deal of capital up front to succeed.

Focusing on the correct capital source and identifying achievable milestones can simplify the capital raising process.

"If you want to be successful, it's just this simple. Know what you are doing. Love what you are doing. And believe in what you are doing."

– *Will Rogers*

THE PLAN

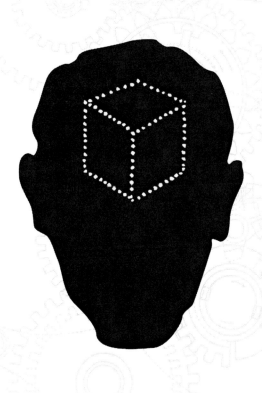

Firing Pulses

A
B
C
A'
B'
C'

4

In recent years, "experts" and pundits have told entrepreneurs that they don't need a business plan. In the words of the Rooster, Foghorn Leghorn, "That's a joke...I say, that's a joke, son." If you plan to ask someone else for money–whether it is a grant, a loan, or an investment–you have to have a well-thought-out, and well-written business plan.

Creating a formal business plan isn't as daunting as it may sound. You will have already drafted many versions of your plan. You can start with the preliminary business plan that was part of your Proof-of-Concept stage as the basis for your Seed Stage plan.

Don't believe it when someone else tells you they will write your business plan. It can't be done. Not only will you really learn your business by writing your plan, you will express your ideas and passion in your own voice and words. You don't have to write it all at once. Break it down into sections and write on it every day. Once you have a solid draft–and this will writing and rewriting, you can engage a professional to edit for you. But only you can write your plan.

Entrepreneurs often ask us for examples of a business plan. We tell them we'll give suggestions and guidelines but not a sample plan. Nor will you will find an example of a business plan in this handbook. Because the most effective business plans we have seen–and we have reviewed thousands of them–are always written by the entrepreneur.

An effective business plan will focus on the business opportunity and outline key milestones to be achieved. The business plan is the all-important first impression for raising money, forming partnerships, and promoting your company.

The business plan reflects all the industry specific information, data, and knowledge you have collected to date. It should accurately reflect your intent, rationale, conclusions, assumptions, and expectations concerning your business venture for the next five years.

The plan will be no more than 10 to 30 pages including financials. We've referred to the entrepreneurial great Guy Kawasaki previously in this book, but again to paraphrase him, "The business plan identifies a problem in the market and a solution to that problem."

The business plan is the product upon which investors will base their decision for present and future funding. It is the road map that will guide the management team for the near future, and which ultimately will be the measure of the businesses performance.

It will take some research and networking to figure out where to send your plan. If there are angel groups in your area, that's a good place to start. Economic development organizations are another source of information. So are service providers such as attorneys and CPAs. The single best way to have a potential investor read your plan is to have it referred by someone they know and trust.

Understand your audience. Friends and family may read or listen with a tolerant ear, but angel investors and venture capitalists are inundated with potential deals.

Angel investors are accustomed to making decisions quickly. The one thing they don't have enough of is time. You have to get their attention in the first three paragraphs of the executive summary, or no matter how fantastic your solution is, they will move on to something else.

While a business plan is undeniably a lot of work, it has benefits beyond the money it raises or commitments it secures. Writing a business plan creates the opportunity for your management team to work together and formally express the intentions of the business.

By the time you've hammered out an effective business plan and the subsequent business presentation, every member of your team understands the opportunities, goals, and risks to the company. There is no single better way to achieve the laser-like focus that you will need to make your venture a success.

OVERVIEW

Writing a business plan is like catching a fish. Most of the work is in the preparation. In researching your market opportunity, you will be learning information—about the market, the competition, and even potential customers that will add depth to your business plan. Be disciplined about collecting, protecting, and categorizing what you learn. When it comes time to write your business plan, you'll have more credibility if you talk about the size of the market *and* what you know about the problem your company is setting out to solve.

First follow the basics:

Target the correct audience.
Focus on the executive summary.
Avoid technical jargon.
Use charts, graphics, headings.
Keep the plan easy to read.
Try to prepare a 15-page plan.
Don't exceed 30 pages.
Hold the financial projections to two to three pages and keep them current, factual, and realistic.

Anticipate and answer the questions investors want to ask. Your audience evaluates business plans all the time. They know the questions, and they've heard most of the answers before. Respect their experience and present the information they want and need to make a decision about whether or not to invest in your company.

- What is the problem you solve?
- What is your solution?
- What is unique about your company that will make it successful?
- What do you know about the market?
- What are the company's goals and how will you achieve them?
- What is the competitive landscape?
- What are the barriers to entry?
- Who is management?
- Why should someone invest in you and your team?
- How are you going to make investors and yourself money?
- What are your assumptions?
- How has the company been funded to date?
- How much money do you need?
- What is your use of funds?

If you answer these questions, you now have a business plan.

There are many business plan tools available. Investigate them. You can save yourself considerable time by choosing a template that relieves you of most of the mechanics of document preparation. There are also online and classroom-based seminars on developing and writing business plans.

We have found the following flow to be an effective organization of a well-written business plan:

Executive Summary

Elevator Pitch

Company Overview and Background

Problem / Solution

Products and Technology

Market Opportunity

Marketing Strategy and Execution

Management Team

Financials, Use of Funds, Investment Strategy

Risk Assessment

Let's proceed with a brief overview of each business plan element.

EXECUTIVE SUMMARY

The Executive Summary is your do-or-die opportunity to grab a potential investor's attention and convince them to read your business plan. Following the same format as the full business plan, cover the major highlights in a two-to three-page detachable document.

It is not at all unusual for active angel groups or venture capitalists to receive a business plan every other day. If you want to earn serious consideration, the story you tell in your Executive Summary must be compelling.

THE ELEVATOR PITCH, COMPANY OVERVIEW AND BACKGROUND

Begin your executive summary with your "Elevator Pitch." The name comes from the idea that a great Elevator Pitch can be delivered between the time the elevator door closes and the passengers reach the next floor.

This is the same carefully crafted statement that you use to verbally describe what your business does and how you plan to make money. It takes about a minute to say. It's three lines long on the page. Rehearse your elevator pitch until you know it better than your own address.

Here are two examples of an Elevator Pitch for the same company.

We produce a disposable, inflatable sleeve for RNs and EMTs to use. It is designed to force blood from deeper tissues into superficial veins.

And

For nurses and emergency personnel that can't find a vein for an IV, we have developed a patented, disposable device that then redirects blood to engorge the vein, making it easier to insert a catheter and might save a life.

Would the first statement give you any idea of what the company does? No. It sounds like industry jargon and gobbledy-gook.

The second statement, however, tells investors exactly what the company is setting out to do. These few lines make you want to read on. It isn't easy to craft executive summaries like these, but if you can't describe your business to strangers who don't understand your technology in a couple of sentences, you are not ready to raise capital.

In the company overview, state the significant milestones the company has achieved to date. Mention strategic partnerships or relationships. You want to convey the founding team's direction and foresight through citing these early results.

Remember, you're trying to attract other people's money. Your suit and hairstyle are not enough. You need to be credible and state your accomplishments to date as well as what you plan to do in the immediate future.

PROBLEM AND SOLUTION

The centerpiece of your business plan is your solution to a big, important problem (current or emerging) and how that solution will generate revenue and profits for your business.

The biggest mistake that entrepreneurs make is failing to invest the time and legwork to understand deeply the markets they are trying to serve. You may have invented or licensed the coolest technology in the world, but unless you match it to a defined market need, technology is just technology.

Before you can figure out a success plan and strategy for your company, you have to understand what your solution can do for the market place. If you are an inquisitive entrepreneur who is willing to ask questions and then be disciplined about organizing and recording what you learn, gaining insight into your potential customers and their problems isn't as difficult or as expensive as you might think.

You are looking for two kinds of information—quantitative information about the size and characteristics of the market and qualitative information from people and companies already in the industry, especially if they might eventually be your customers.

There's no substitute for what an entrepreneur can learn from direct conversations with human beings. Call some customers you think your idea could help. People like to talk about their problems; you might be surprised what you will learn. Call experts in the field. Use your community contacts or college professors. Trade, product, and industry associations are excellent sources of information.

Whether you are a member or not, executive directors and other association leaders will often take your call. Consider attending major industry shows or trade events. Government departments, non-profit economic agencies, and entrepreneur centers often have extensive online archives or resource libraries.

Use what you learn to explain how your product or service will solve the problems that the people you met and talked to have. Explain your value proposition—why customers need your product or service and why they will be willing to pay for it.

What is it about your solution that creates high future demand?

Nothing catches an investor's attention more than evidence that an entrepreneur has listened to many customers in the markets into which he or she intends to sell.

PRODUCTS AND TECHNOLOGY

Cover only the important aspects of the product. This is not the time to go overboard writing about your product or technology, as innovative and wonderful as it may be.

Some form of intellectual property (IP) is almost always at the foundation of any scalable technology entrepreneurial venture. Patents can add to the asset value of the company, and investors want to know that IP is appropriately protected, whether through patents or other methods. Discuss how you will create a sustainable competitive barrier in addition to any IP.

Emphasize any unique features or competitive advantages and how these produce benefits for the end user. Potential investors know that for a product or service to succeed in the marketplace, it must be less expensive or better performing than the competition, or must be able to solve a problem that couldn't be solved before. Show how your customers will use your product and why they would be willing to pay for it.

Include clear and straightforward diagrams to help the reader. Test the effectiveness of your explanation on your non-technical friends. Can they read this section of your plan and understand what you are talking about? If not, rewrite.

MARKET OPPORTUNITY

You have demonstrated your knowledge of the market, outlined the problem, and emphasized your solution. Now is the time to use your crystal ball to speculate on the long-term growth prospects of the market and your company.

The quantitative information that you collected helps qualify the market and develops a level of confidence about the marketability of the product. Your assessment of who will buy your product, how many of those buyers exist, and how much they will pay makes up the Market Opportunity statement in your business plan. Focus on the markets that you intend to serve. Investors look for a company that knows how to narrow the focus and prioritize.

Cite third-party research—but only those statistics that are relevant to your business. You will be using data primarily from secondary sources such as trade journals, periodicals, existing market studies, and electronic data. Make sure it is the most current available. Keep an accurate record of your sources.

Internet search engines can become your best friend to find specific facts as well as market trends. Outline the size and growth trends of your target market. If you have interest from companies or customers, now is the time to talk about it.

All businesses have competition. Understand yours—those who are already selling to the industry and those who might enter the market in the future. Analyze their pricing and products. Don't neglect that nemesis of many new companies—the inertia of the status quo.

MARKETING STRATEGY AND EXECUTION

The goal is to illustrate how you will attack the market and produce revenue. The operational strategies that you express are keys to the execution of the overall business mission.

Identify early market niches or "early adopters," customers who are innovative or who are in such pain that they would be likely to take a risk on your solution sooner. Most customers don't move fast, especially when it comes to adopting a new technology or process. Identify and then create a strategy to get to the easy ones first.

What is your pricing strategy? Will customers license your technology? Do you plan to follow the software as a service (SaaS) model and charge by the month or by the click? Will you have a base offering with additional features priced separately or tiered pricing aimed at specific markets? How do your competitors price?

As part of your business plan process, be prepared to make an investment in branding. Your brand encompasses your company name, logo, tagline, Web site, and any marketing collaterals.

You don't need to come up with a logo as recognizable as the Nike swoosh, but your logo and company name do need to serve you for three to five years. They are part of the quality image you want to project.

Be prepared to spend some of your carefully conserved cash on these items. This is not the time to hire your cousin to save a few dollars unless your cousin is an expert in design.

Outline your marketing, sales, and promotional strategy. Articulate the company's partnering goals. Although your company is young, your product is still under development, and you probably don't have any customers yet, there are cost-effective ways to gain early recognition in the marketplace.

Volunteer to speak at your local Chamber or as a guest presenter in college or graduate-level entrepreneurial classes. When you see an article in a local paper, magazine, or on a web site that is in your field, call the author, and volunteer to contribute to his or her next piece about your industry. Send out press releases. Include copies of anything written about you or your company as an addendum to the marketing section of your plan.

If you plan to develop an in-house sales force, be prepared to address training and after sales support. If your plan is to sell through other organizations, identify the channels you seek as partners, your plan for convincing them to partner with you, and why they would want to say yes.

Include a chart of key milestones for the next six to 24 months. Repeat...include a chart.

MANAGEMENT TEAM

Investors invest in people first and technology second. List your team's depth and experience to demonstrate your worthiness and credibility. Include a paragraph for each key executive that covers all relevant experience. Investors want to know if you've worked together before and how you operate as a team. Emphasize all experience in the target industry as well as key relationships with potential clients or suppliers.

Acknowledge the limitations of the founding staff in relation to the future company. If you are a technical professional without much operating experience, as many founding entrepreneurs are, anticipate the need for skills that you don't have. Summarize key hires for immediate, intermediate, and longer-term time frames. Keep your ego out of the discussion. Do not fill a position with a weak candidate just to avoid a hole in the team. You can do a lot, but investors know that you can't do everything.

FINANCIALS, USE OF FUNDS, INVESTMENT STRATEGY

The financials are driven by the marketing strategy and milestones. Clearly state all assumptions and tie them back to the milestones of the marketing plan. Represent a complete set of financials in two to three pages covering three to five years, including a current income statement, balance sheet, and cash flow statement.

Always use a "bottom up" approach based on your market intelligence. Never use a "top down" analysis...and most important, never, ever tell investors that your company only needs "1, 2, or even 5 percent market share" to achieve your revenue goals.

For many entrepreneurs understanding how to construct and explain the financials is challenging. If you don't have an undergraduate degree in business or an MBA, get some help in this important area. The founder of a company cannot expect to delegate the financials and succeed.

**Include the following financial information in your
business plan.**

- Assets and liabilities
- Sales volumes
- Operating expenses
- Net income and cash flow
- Gross margin
- Revenue growth

If you don't already understand what each of these terms
means and how to calculate it, find a tutor. Without this
understanding you can't create a business plan, but more
importantly, you can't create a company.

Be specific about the funding you will need. Tie capital
requirements to milestone accomplishments. If you expect
to need multiple rounds of funding, make the amounts and
timing clear. Valuation of your business is a cornerstone of
your financial projections and is the subject of Chapter 7.

- Details of investment opportunity
- Funds sought
- Form of investment
- Pre/Post money valuation
- Ownership Percentage
- Subsequent funding required
- Use of funds, Exit Strategies, and Return on Investment

No matter what your financial projections are, they will be wrong. Potential investors know this. They want to see if you recognize the importance of managing cost while driving toward break-even.

UNDERSTANDING AND EXPRESSING THE RISK IN YOUR BUSINESS PLAN

Experienced investors know that there is risk in your business plan. They want to know that you know this, too. Entrepreneurs are by nature optimistic, can-do types. Identify the risky areas of your plan, and then have strategies to compensate or overcome that risk.

The following checklist is a risk assessment tool. Follow the thought process presented in Chapter 2 to ensure that every item below is clearly communicated and addressed in your plan as an integral part of your business strategy. Each of these lines is a question that you must be able to answer.

The goal of this exercise isn't to scare you off. It is to help you create a sound business plan that you and potential investors can have confidence in...knowing that surprises and changes are likely to happen every step of the way.

This process helps you, the entrepreneur, keep your eye on the ball of the critical corporate challenge to be faced in a very tumultuous time.

BUSINESS MODEL RISK

- Primary business risks and credible strategies for addressing these risks
- The company's value proposition
- Customer's ROI
- Gross profit of the company
- Strategies and use of investment funds
- Path to break even and profitability
- Highlights and substantiates the "competitive barriers"
- Below-market cash compensation to management pre-profit
- Milestones will change the value of the company when achieved relative to operational

TECHNOLOGY/PRODUCT RISK

- Product status- conceptual, working model, prototype, production prototype
- Description of level of complexity of the product
- Is the product evolutionary, disruptive, or revolutionary?
- Product testing in the user environment
- Does the product integrate in the current market environment or does it require market education, user education?
- Competitive or unique features of the product
- Competitive technological barriers, such as patents, long developmental cycles, or trademarks
- Expected life cycle of the product
- Multiple products or lines of revenue relative to life cycle
- Continuing research and development

MARKET RISK

- Explain the current market and how it may change
- Market trends
- Market size and market growth rates for each product/service
- Potential early adopters
- Logical prioritization of product/service launches derived from the Sales or testing that includes user responses as to price, features, and satisfaction
- Defensible pricing strategy validated with customer surveys
- Customer data from surveys or interviews that supports their projected sales volumes and price points
- Competitive analysis to include strengths/weaknesses comparison chart
- Market relationships developed
- Why, how, and where the customer will purchase
- A detailed plan to develop access to critical distribution channels, whether a direct sales force, product representatives, resellers, or value add resellers
- Future plans for incremental products/services

EXECUTION RISK

- Experience and strength of proven management team presented in biography format
- Appropriate and diversity of skill sets, relevant managerial experience, industry knowledge
- Experience in commercializing new products and/or developing new businesses
- Staffing matched to the company's stage of commercialization
- Time line for critical hires matched to milestone events
- Management compensation structured for a short- and

long-term sustainability with annual base salaries below
market and supported by an annual cash bonus pool
based upon achievement of specific quantified milestones
- Entire management team owns or has stock options
- External service providers to cost effectively supplement
and provide the necessary skills that aren't in-house
- Board of Directors includes external representation, and
ideally control with capacity to provide accessibility
to key customers, industry knowledge, managerial
experience, and/or capital sources
- Use of advisory committees and/or mentors

FINANCE RISK

- Concise financial projections including income
statement, balance sheet, and cash flows
- Stated assumptions and justification for the revenue and
gross profit outlooks
- Financial assumptions included based on market and
sales forecasts
- Source and use of funds with impact analysis of higher or
lower funding
- Corporate benefit associated with each capital expenditure
- Substantial economic investment by founders and/or
management
- Reasonable, justifiable valuation stating rational and approach
- Current capital market valuations specifically for companies
of a similar risk profile and/or stage of commercialization
- Preferred stock, board seats and employee stock option
pools
- Anticipated subsequent financing rounds until company
reaches break-even and is self-supporting with cash flow

- Exit strategies and rationale for each
- Strategies to achieve investors' ROI of at least 30 percent and more than 30 times (30 X) money over expected holding period

To include or not to include the risk assessment in your plan is the question. The information in a formatted way certainly shows your credibility.

CONCLUSION

Guess what? Once you complete the plan, it will be time to update it again!

Technologists create innovative products and technologies. Business people turn technologies into successful companies.

A thoroughly researched and expressed business plan is your opportunity to credibly demonstrate that you understand your market and can solve a problem for potential customers.

No entrepreneur can ever know too much about the competition. Clear language and well-documented hands-on market research make it easy for potential investors to consider your business plan.

KEY POINTS

The executive summary is the all-important first impression for raising money, forming partnerships, and promoting your company.

Writing an effective, formal business plan isn't as daunting as it sounds.

Ask others for advice, but write your plan yourself. Not only will you really learn your business, you will express your ideas and passion in your own voice and words.

An effective business plan focuses on the business opportunity and outlines key milestones to be achieved.

Understand your audience.

Do research and networking to figure out where to send your plan to get the best results.

Keep it short. All that's needed is ten to 30 pages.

"Never miss a good chance to shut up."

– Will Rogers

THE PITCH

5

You have emailed your business plans to dozens of angel investors. You've networked wisely with local contacts and are planning for success.

Your elevator pitch and executive summary have provided the opportunity for you to share your business plan. Your business plan has opened the door for you to provide a proven pitch of your business opportunity.

When the opportunity to make a formal business plan pitch arrives, you want to be ready with a thoughtful and well-rehearsed pitch.

The primary audience for your pitch is investors, although, as you progress through the stages of the Entrepreneurial Path, you can adapt your pitch to multiple audiences, including business partners, economic development organizations, and even customers.

When you have the opportunity to make your pitch to potential investors, you must capture their attention in the first minute that you speak. People with money to invest in startup businesses are besieged with "deal flow," a steady stream of business plans and opportunities to invest.

You want your pitch to grab them from the very start and make them eager to learn more about your company, your market, and your management team. The quality of the business opportunity, product, and management team are often judged by the quality of the business plan pitch. If this is beginning to feel like a make-or-break event, that's because it is.

An effective business plan pitch takes 17 to 20 minutes with 16 slides or less. Skip the dramatics. This is not the time to come up with some gimmick. Be enthusiastic and passionate, but never theatrical.

Begin your pitch by telling a story about the problem that your product or service solves. This will grab investors' attention and don't let go. Figure out a way to put your audience in the shoes of someone who will benefit from your product or service. Your goal is to help investors get a picture in their heads about the problem you are solving.

From coaching hundreds of entrepreneurs, we have developed a pitch template and roadmap that kicks off with the Elevator Pitch and concludes with an assessment of the company exit that delivers on investors' desired financial return.

When an entrepreneur really understands his or her business plan, has prepared for questions, and feels confident and comfortable without feeling arrogant, they get better results.

We recommend the following content and order for your business plan pitch. Whatever format you choose, make sure it is consistent with your business plan format.

Title Slide

Market Problem

Your Solution

Business Model and Sales

Market Demand

Competition

Growth Opportunity

Management Team

Financial Projections

Financial Projections Chart

Investment Strategy and Use of Funds

Company Milestones

Milestones – Past & Future Business & Financial

Valuation Chart

Risk Assessment

Exit Strategy

Following is a slide by slide discussion of the content of your pitch.

TITLE SLIDE AND ELEVATOR PITCH

Use *less than two* minutes to position the company to the audience. Introduce yourself and your title. State the name of your company, and give the one sentence version of your Elevator Pitch to excite people and provide a quick and concise understanding of your business. Share the company history and why you are there.

 It's so easy to spend too much time on the opening slide. Anticipate and resist this temptation. Do not spend more than one minute, tops. You have less than 20 minutes for your entire pitch. Resist squandering your time.

MARKET PROBLEM

Clearly communicate the "problem" in the market to lay the foundation for the slides that will follow. Provide two examples that will relate to the "unfair" advantage that your solution has.

YOUR SOLUTION

Describe how you know there is a problem or pain in the market. This is the place to share your personal experience from talking with customers. Be sparing, but sprinkle it in. This adds credibility and demonstrates your knowledge of the market needs. What is the problem costing the market? This sets up the value proposition for your solution, which you will present in the next slide.

Describe the essence of your product or technology and how it solves the current problem in the marketplace. You are the doctor–how do you ease the financial or physical pain?

Summarize your solution emphasizing the uniqueness of your product or technology, but DO NOT get mired in the "gee-whiz." Your audience wants to know how you have protected the intellectual property, but at this point, they do not need to know about the details of the technology.

Outline the return on investment (ROI) that your solution offers the customers and how long it will take them to recoup their investment. Focus on the benefits to the customer.

BUSINESS MODEL

Describe how your product or service generates revenue for your company. Does it follow the software as a service (SaaS) model? Do you charge licensing fees? Is it purchase only? The more simplistic the business model, the better. Express your sales and channel strategy. How do you plan to reach initial customers? Do you plan to sell direct? Are there existing distribution channels that would be a good fit for partnering with you?

MARKET DEMAND

Explain why someone would want to pay for your solution. Quantify the estimated market size, including prospective customers, especially early adopters; market segments, and potential sales revenues, but don't get all wrapped up in sky-high numbers. Characterize the key attributes of target customers. Talk about your first-hand experience and explain the reason for market growth over the next three to five years.

COMPETITION

Create a comparison guide of competitors so that your audience can see the landscape at a glance. Include the better funded and more well-known large companies as well as smaller innovative competitors. Don't ignore competitors who have a partial solution. Describe your company's strongest barriers to competitive threats. Be clear about what it will take to get customers to change what they are doing today. Inertia is sometimes the fiercest competitor!

GROWTH OPPORTUNITY

Demonstrate the company growth potential after initial launch. Specify what needs to happen to produce positive cash flow using milestone examples. Use your research and knowledge of the market to illustrate the characteristics of your key market segments, and the nature of market growth. Show the urgency of the need for the product or service you will supply.

MANAGEMENT TEAM

Investors know that execution is everything. You will often hear investors say that they prefer to invest in an "A" management team and a "B" product rather than the other way around. Experience in the target market, growing sales, building teams, and managing capital is a must.

This is your moment to show how strong your team is individually **and** to demonstrate how well you work together as a team. Describe your board of directors and/or advisors, highlighting their strategic value. Use concise bullet points to describe experience. Indicate who is full-time and who is part-time.

CEO: Prior entrepreneurial experience and/or years in a similar business or market

CTO or CMO: Track record in core product or technology area; knowledge of target markets and relationship with the industry

CFO: Prior experience including acquisitions and other exit events.

Identify technical or business advisors, mentors or members of your board of directors and the experience and skills they possess that supplement internal skills.

FINANCIAL PROJECTIONS

Focus on the bottom line. State the amount of capital needed to reach breakeven and profitability. Project realistic revenues. Expect to explain short-term market adoption and penetration, dramatic or hockey stick growth, margins beyond the norm, and any extended periods of negative cash flow.

Chart 5.1
Financial Projections

	Latest Actual Financials	Proected Year 1	Projected Year 2	Projected Year 3	Projected Year 4	Projected Year 5
Revenue ($)	128	1,200	5,400	13,600	24,300	36,000
Costs of Goods Sold ($)	82	650	2,200	5,200	9,100	13,300
Gross Profit ($)	46	550	3,200	8,400	15,200	22,700
Gross Profit %	35.9%	45.8%	59.3%	61.8%	62.6%	63.1%
Operations/G&A ($)	151	540	1,780	3,600	6,300	8,100
Income/Loss before Tax ($)	(105)	10	1,420	4,800	8,900	14,600
Inc./Loss before Tax%	-82.0	0.8%	26.3%	35.3%	36.6%	40.6%

INVESTMENT STRATEGY

It is always smart to include a Capitalization Table. This is a table that represents who owns what percentage of the new company. If your company hasn't received equity capital yet, this will be a picture of founders, friends, and family investments and percentages of ownership.

As you bring on investment capital, it is always important to keep your Capitalization Table up to date. For presentation purposes, you can list investors by group.

Split your future capital needs into the appropriate rounds matching the key milestones to be achieved. Highlight in a sentence or two the risks associated with those potential milestones. Your goal is to present an optimistic *and* realistic view as you see it today.

USE OF FUNDS/VALUATION

Identify the current burn rate. Identify the major uses of funds for each round up to acquisition or alternate exit scenario. Use of funds should focus on revenue-generating activities or key technical and product development milestones.

Include a valuation chart, which you will understand much better after you complete Chapter 6. Be prepared for tough questioning if your company pre-money valuation exceeds a normal range for the current stage of your company.

Chart 5.2
Use of Funds/Valuation/Investment Strategy

	Pre-Money Valuation	Amount of Funding Sought	Post-Money Valuaiton	Founders	Seed Round Investors	VC Round 1 Investors	VC Round 2 Investors
Seed Round ($)	1,250,000	500,000	1,750,000	1,250,000 71.4%	500,000 28.6%		
VC Round ($)	3,000,000	1,500,000	4,500,000	2,142,857 47.6%	857,143 19.0%	1,500,000 33.3%	
VC Round 2 ($)	4,500,000	2,000,000	6,500,000	2,142,857 33.0%	857,143 13.2%	1,500,000 80.1%	2,000,000 30.8%

COMPANY MILESTONES

Provide a milestone chart-at-a-glance that illustrates past and future business and financial accomplishments. These milestones relate directly to the use of funds and investment strategy material presented in your previous charts.

Key milestones to include are company formation, technology or product achievements, past and future rounds of capital, positive cash flow, break-even point, and exit event.

Chart 5.3
Milestones

	2006			2007			2008			2009		
	Jan – Mar	Mar – July	July – Dec	Jan – Mar	Mar – July	July – Dec	Jan – Mr	Mar – July	July – Dec	Jan – Mar	Mar – July	July – Dec
Company Formed	●											
$250K Proof-of-concept	●											
Product Prototype		●										
$400K Seed Round		●										
Field tests		●										
$500K Angel Round			●									
1st Production Ship			●									
Positive Cash Flow				●								
$2M VC Round					●							
50M Annualized Revenue						●						
IPO/Acquisition											●	

RISK ASSESSMENT

It is no surprise to investors that entrepreneurial businesses are risky. They want to know that you have realistically analyzed your business opportunity with respect to the key areas of risk. Share your assessment honestly. Tell them what keeps you up at night. Follow the risk segmentation process presented in Chapter 2 of this guide according to product, market, business, finance, and execution risk. Be open and candid about the technical development sales cycle, anticipated adoption rate, cash flows, personnel, competition, and costs.

EXIT STRATEGY/LIQUIDITY

There are three primary positive options for an exit or liquidity event– acquisition, Initial Public Offering (IPO), or fire sale. The third option is definitely not fun! Investors are not interested in being part of the company for life.

Demonstrate that while your interest is in building a viable business, you understand that your investors are looking for an exit and return in three to five years. Express the value proposition for the investors in each of the exit scenarios you discuss. How do they get their money back and what is their return?

There are very, very few IPOs these days. Demonstrate that you understand and accept this reality of the marketplace. If there are any specifics of how acquisition and IPO might apply to your company, share those briefly.

For the acquisition discussion, identify at least two of the most likely buyers and why they would be interested. Describe recent comparable transactions and value. List any relationships that are currently in place between yourself or your company and potential acquirers.

Bite Your Tongue! Things you never ever want to say!
- *This is the best deal you will ever see.*
- *No one else does what we do.*
- *We are chasing billion dollar markets.*
- *Our intellectual property is solid.*
- *We don't have any competition.*
- *Big corporations are too slow to be a threat.*
- *Our financial projections are conservative.*
- *We need 1 percent market share to meet our projections, which are conservative.*
- *Our margins exceed 10 percent.*
- *A big corporate partner is about to sign on.*
- *Key employees will join us at funding.*
- *Revenues are not our current focus.*

And our favorite...
- *Several angels and VCs are interested in funding our plan.*

PITCH RULES

Ahead of Time

- Allow a reference to arrange the meeting.
- Rehearse, rehearse, and rehearse!
- Target the right audience; there are big differences between partners, angels and venture capitalists.
- Practice your pitch skills, limit use of the word "um."
- Use four bullets per page, four words per bullet.
- Avoid anything other than simple pictures, graphics and extremely abbreviated text.
- Test your pitch technology ahead of time and onsite.
- Read *The Art of the Start*, by Guy Kawasaki

Pitch Day

- Show up early and bring only key personnel.
- Wear business attire; no flip-flops or casual dress.
- Be enthusiastic but not annoying.
- Use appropriate social skills, no off-color jokes.
- Express appreciation for the audience's time and interest.
- Keep a pen and note pad handy.

Your Delivery

- Don't read to the audience.
- Don't be dramatic or theatrical.
- Let the audience know how your business makes money.
- You must be knowledgeable of the subject presented.
- Be prepared to answer questions.
- Be open to audience recommendations.
- Demonstrate that you are a "coachable" entrepreneur.

Be Prepared to Answer These Questions

- What problem does your company solve?
- What is the market potential for your product/ service?
- Who is the target user of the product or service offering?
- Why would they purchase your product or service?
- How do you plan to acquire and keep customers?
- Does the company have proprietary intellectual property?
- What makes your business different or unique?
- Who are your competitors?
- What gives your company a competitive advantage?
- What is it about your management team that makes them uniquely capable of executing on this business plan?
- What is the planned "use of funds"?
- When will the company reach breakeven?
- What are the primary risks facing your business opportunity?
- What are the exit scenarios for the founders and investors?

CONCLUSION

How you deliver your pitch is as important as what you say. Your pitch must educate and sell, and it's up to you to achieve the appropriate balance of both. Demonstrate your passion for your business, your customers, and the potential of the marketplace.

Practice, practice, and then practice some more. In front of the mirror, in front of your family, friends, and employees. Seek the advice of mentors and other professionals. Learn from each experience.

Seek out opportunities to talk about your company to an audience before you have the opportunity to present to investors. The practice is invaluable, and you will learn from this experience where you need to improve.

You will learn from the questions your audience does or doesn't ask whether your pitch is a success—and when it is, that's just the beginning. There will be weeks of due diligence and additional pitches before you and potential investors sit down to terms. That's the subject of the next chapter.

KEY POINTS

When the opportunity to make a formal business plan presentation arrives, you want to be ready with a thoughtful and well-rehearsed pitch.

The quality of the business opportunity, product, and management team are often judged by the quality of the business plan pitch.

An effective business plan presentation takes 17 to 20 minutes with 16 slides or less.

The primary audience for your pitch is investors, although, you can adapt your presentation to multiple audiences.

If you don't communicate anything else, create a picture in your audience's minds about how your product or service solves a huge problem or pain in the marketplace.

"It's not what you pay a man, but what he costs you that counts."

– Will Rogers

THE PRICE

ST PAT NO. A 800328

Every entrepreneur will be faced with the task of valuing his or her company. The initial valuation process occurs at a critical time in a company's life, because it reflects the first time that investment capital is received.

Some people advise entrepreneurs to wait on valuation discussion until an investor brings up the topic. We advise and invest in so many companies each year that we prefer to introduce valuation in the beginning.

The valuation process and results have both immediate and long-term impacts on the company founder and investors. Valuation affects how much of the company the founder must give up in return for much-needed capital. And, as important as the financial considerations are, valuation negotiations often set the tone of the relationship between entrepreneur and investors for the months and years ahead.

By seeking a valuation that is too high or unrealistic, the entrepreneur risks losing the interest of investors entirely. For example, if the investor has market intelligence that shows a company should have a $2 million valuation and the entrepreneur is expecting a $10 million valuation, then the distance is too far to traverse and the parties will walk away.

Valuation also affects the investors' return on their investment (ROI) and may affect the company's ability to raise additional capital in follow-on rounds.

We've seen numerous companies ultimately fail because the financial composition is such that it makes no sense for existing or new investors to put more capital in the

company. This happens often times due to high valuation
early in the company's life.

*The better an entrepreneur understands
how valuation works and how to assess the
current and future value of his or her share
of the company as the business grows, the
more informed, effective, and mutually
beneficial the process of evaluation will be
for investors and entrepreneurs.*

VOCABULARY OF VALUATION

The valuation process has its own vocabulary. Stay with it
until you really understand. Don't be shy about asking a
more experienced entrepreneur, an attorney, or CPA to help
you become more knowledgeable.

The resources on the Web have never been more in-depth and
plentiful. Visit the Web site of the Angel Capital Education
Foundation (ACEF), a charitable organization devoted the
education, information, and research about angel investing.
ACEF is a good source of white papers and articles that
explain valuation. (www.angelcapitaleducation.org/about-acef/)

The following example demonstrates the basics of
valuation. For purposes of valuation, the value of the
venture has three components:

Pre-money valuation - the value of the company prior
to investment. This amount considers items such as
cash; patents; inventory; property and equipment, and
receivables, net of liabilities.

Post-money – equals the pre-money value + investment amount

New Investment – The amount of capital the company is raising during this round.

NOW LET'S WORK THE MATH

Assume that your company has a valuation of $ 1,000,000 and you are the only shareholder.

You sell 33 percent of your company to investors to raise $500,000 in a Series A round.

The original shareholder (you) now owns 66.67 percent of the company that is now worth $1,500,000. The new investors own 33.3 percent.

Pre-money valuation:	$ 1,000,000
Investment amount:	$ 500,000
Post-money valuation:	$ 1,500,000

Your 66.67 percent share of the post-money valuation of the company is worth $1,000,000.

The above post-money valuation ($1,500,000) becomes the new pre-money valuation. If follow-on rounds of capital are sought, a new pre-money valuation will be negotiated each time. If you receive a Series B investment, you *and* your Series A will now give up a portion of your Series A valuation in return for additional investment capital.

Just as the value of the original shareholder's (you) 66.67 percent share was diluted in the Series A round, in a Series B round, the shares of the previous owners (You and the Series A investors) will be **diluted** (or worth less) if they don't invest their pro-rate share of the next investment.

Dilution is when the addition to the number of shares outstanding reduces the value of holdings of existing shareholder. Everyone now owns a smaller percentage of the total. However, if the value of the company increased, your value or worth has increased.

When a company's pre-money value is *less* than its post-money value *after* the round of financing, it is known as a down round. Down rounds are frequent, but not good.

In a **Down Round** of financing, the previous investors' share of the business is diluted much more than normal because the original investment was closed at too high a valuation. This fatigues investors. The key is for the entrepreneur to be reasonable in the beginning when they are raising capital, and recognize that it is hard work to increase valuation.

THE DEMAND FOR CAPITAL GREATLY EXCEEDS THE SUPPLY

There is a direct relationship between the stage of the Entrepreneurial Path and the company's valuation.

A Seed Stage company has a proven concept. A Start-up Stage business has a service or product in development.

An Early Stage company has beta tests, and perhaps a thin revenue stream from some early adopters. In other words, market validation.

By definition Seed and Startup Stage companies don't have revenue or, if they do, not enough to be a determining factor. This makes the initial valuation at these critical stages more an art than science.

 You will be better prepared to value your company, after you consider valuation from the investors' point of view. First of all, give up your belief that angels and venture capitalists love risk. They don't. It is returns on their investment that they like.

If angel investors invest $500,000 in your business, they will be seeking a $2 to $5 million return over the next three to five years as a reward for their risk, depending on the investment stage. In the earlier, more risky stages of the company, angels will seek the highest returns.

If they don't believe your business has the potential for that, angels will move on to the next entrepreneur. Even interested investors don't share the same enthusiasm as entrepreneurs, so the entrepreneur's projections are heavily discounted. As innovative as your technology may be, the value of a technology has little relevance on the value of the company until it is commercialized into a product that begins producing revenue or until it has been developed to the point that another company will acquire it.

Further, angel investors know that almost every company will have unforeseen future capital needs. Unexpected future investments dilute the percentage of ownership of existing investors and founders.

APPROACH TO VALUATION

A common pitfall that many Seed, Startup, and Early Stage entrepreneurs make is over-valuing their companies. This drives investors away.

If you do raise money at a too-high valuation, you are endangering the ability of the company to raise capital in the future because a too high valuation early requires too much work and headache to correct later.

There are multiple methods for determining the value of a company. Comparing multiple methods can be beneficial for Seed, Startup, and Early Stage ventures.

Throughout the process, don't lose sight of this reality—that you are trying determine a value for a company that has no revenue, no track record of sales, and few if any customers. You can create scenarios, but you do not and cannot know what will actually happen in the market place.

VALUATION MODELS AND METHODS

Increasingly, valuation is determined by national and international capital markets, not based on regionalism. Draw comparable values for your business from national sources as early in the life of the company as possible.

Three useful valuation methods for an entrepreneur to consider are **comparable private transactions**, **comparable public transactions**, and **net present value (NPV) of discounted cash flows**.

COMPARABLE PRIVATE TRANSACTIONS

Using recent private venture transactions that are comparable in market sector, stage of company, and local and national investment markets is the best approach. This method illustrates a quantitative state of the market and helps determine the current investment market price. This is the best approach for the proof-of-concept, seed, and early stage companies.

It is difficult to identify comparables because valuation is rarely disclosed on these deals. Your best sources are the Internet, other entrepreneurs, and support organizations. Prepare to spend days Googling.

Investors will have more comparables on valuation because they are constantly looking at new deals. They may also have invested in other "comparable" deals which can influence their view of valuation of your deal.

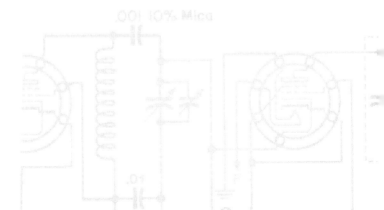

Other sources are Dow Jones VentureSource, (www. dowjones.com/privatemarkets/venturesource.asp), Pricewaterhouse Cooper Money Tree (www.pwcmoneytree. com/MTPublic/ns/index.jsp), press releases, and the entrepreneurial community.

COMPARABLE PUBLIC TRANSACTIONS

Public transactions can be a good source of comparable information. If the company is truly comparable, assessing the valuation and multiples and making comparisons with other companies that have been acquired can provide a quantitative view of the values that the public market gives to certain levels of profits and revenue.

Public transactions reflect values at the company's exit, so for a company that is in the earlier stages of the Entrepreneurial path, values must be discounted heavily to arrive at a proxy for current value. Potential dilution must also be factored in. These considerations and calculations are complex, especially for first-time entrepreneurs. Find someone to tutor you.

This valuation analysis must be discounted heavily based on the stage of growth, company management, and liquidity.

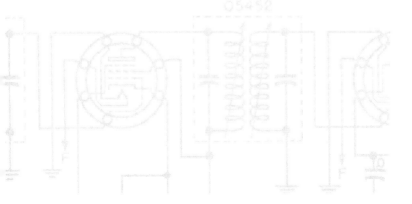

The public market rapidly fluctuates and entrepreneurs often select high-profile, successful companies as the benchmark, when these firms and the conditions of their success aren't actually comparable. Internet business search sites and business publications are sources for identifying companies. The SEC's EDGAR database is a great source for comparables.

NET PRESENT VALUE (NPV)
OF DISCOUNTED CASH FLOWS

It is difficult to use the net present value methodology effectively until a company has a history of sales. Without several quarters of sales performance, the analysis will be based entirely on assumptions.

For these reasons, the value of this methodology increases as the company moves from Early into Growth Stage, progressing to later rounds of financing.

It is still a good idea to apply the methodology to your business projects when you are in Startup and Early Stages. It will help you become familiar with the variables and someone may ask for it. We never do, as there is too much guess work involved.

For companies that are in the Growth Stage and beyond, NPV can be very robust if analysis is based on actual revenue and profit results compared to projections.

INVESTORS HOLD THE PURSE

If it's beginning to feel like angels and other early stage investors have the upper hand in valuation, that's because in a sense they do. They possess the money and the experience. They understand the risk. They know first-hand that most entrepreneurial companies need more time and money to reach breakeven than most entrepreneurs expect.

When it all is said and done, many entrepreneurs face the choice of accepting a pre-money valuation on initial funding in the $1 million to $2 million range or continuing on unfunded with a valuation of $3 million or more.

The old adage still holds true: Do you want all of a small pie or part of a bigger pie? It's your choice.

Assuming you are an entrepreneur who wants to achieve the funding necessary for your company to gain stability and grow, you can raise your odds of success by understanding your potential investors' point of view before the valuation process begins. Remember, you are not the only company out raising capital. Your valuation must be competitive.

INVESTMENT RETURN ANALYSIS

All investors expect a return on investment (ROI) in proportion to the level of risk assumed at each stage of capital. Early stage investments are higher risk and require higher returns.

It is good for the entrepreneur to go through this simple analysis. It helps put into perspective the valuation expectations, investors' return expectations, and the amount of capital being raised by the company.

Years ago we ran across an investment return analysis that easily articulated investors' perspectives. Here's the idea. Let's assume:

- Seed investors require 20 times (20X) their investment
- Series A investors require 10 times (10X) their investment
- Series B investors requires five times (5X) their investment

A simple graph of these return requirements **(Chart 6.1)** can illustrate the performance expected from the company. A company that raises $10 million over several stages, including founder's investment, will have set a return expectation of nearly $100 million.

As you review this graph, keep in mind the Entrepreneurial Path that we've outlined in this handbook. Each stage in the path requires a certain type of investor. The following analysis illustrates the expected returns from the company to investors at various stages along the path presuming the company raises $10 million over several stages.

Chart 6.1
Investment Return Analysis

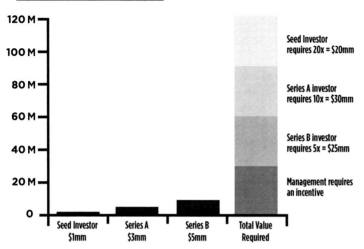

THE FOUNDING TEAM AND MANAGEMENT
DESERVE A PAYOUT, TOO

Entrepreneurs take risk, too. They work 60 to 100 hour
weeks for months on end with little financial reward. They,
too, are looking for substantial rewards at acquisition or
IPO. In fact, angel investors will tell you that when deals
are done right, entrepreneurs always put significantly more
money in their bank accounts than the angel investors do.

There are ways for an entrepreneur to look at valuation,
other than percentage of company ownership. How much
wealth would make you happy when you sell your very first
company?

Dreams of $50 or $100 million IPOs or acquisitions are
wonderful, but for most entrepreneurs, especially if it is

their first venture, these dreams are simply dreams. A more realistic expectation is receiving $1 million to $5 million dollars, and when you think about it, that's not a bad return for three to five years work.

 Think about it. $3 million invested at 4 percent in tax-free bonds generates $10,000 a month without touching principal. This amount of money can support your lifestyle while you find your next startup idea.

Once you decide the lowest level of payout that would delight you, be candid about this with interested investors. Figure out what your company has to accomplish in three to five years to attract a buyer who will acquire your company at a price that will make your financial goal a reality. Then calculate the amount of investment capital (and therefore the valuation) necessary to reach your goals.

THE IMPORTANCE OF BUILDING GOOD RELATIONSHIPS WITH INVESTORS

Entrepreneurs and their investors will need to work together to build and grow a successful company that solves problems for customers, provides jobs for employees, profits for the enterprise, and financial returns for the founder and investors.

 As you build your company, you will depend on your investors for more than the money they invested. They will be members of your board. They likely have Blackberrys and iPhones full of useful contacts. They will influence and likely participate in future investment rounds. It is critical to the success of the company that your interests are aligned.

If you believe your investors are coldheartedly out to take
what is rightfully yours, and if they think you are greedy
and unrealistic about the appropriate return for investing in
your risky enterprise, you will shortchange your company,
your team, and yourself.

TERM SHEETS

The goal for entrepreneurs and investors is to achieve
reasonable and balanced terms that appropriately match the
agreed upon valuation of the early stage company with returns
and protections given the risk. When term sheet negotiations
go badly or fall apart, it is usually caused by inappropriate
expectations.

A realistic approach is to compare the future expectations
of what the company will accomplish with the company's
accomplishments so far. Is the product on schedule? Are
there customers who have committed to become early
adopters? Are key employees on board? Once an investor
buys into the company's projections, those projects become
the basis for the terms.

There are as many versions of term sheets as there are
investors and attorneys. We have seen seven-page term
sheets and term sheets with 30 pages or more. It's never too
soon for an entrepreneur who plans to be successful to learn
about the elements that commonly appear in term sheets.

While the particulars of term sheets will vary, you can expect
every set of terms to address these areas: timing of the release
of funds, anti-dilution terms, liquidation preferences, voting

and redemptive rights, and board of directors' seats. These provisions are complicated beyond the scope of this handbook.

However, they potentially have such an impact on the entrepreneur's financial future that we introduce the concepts here and encourage you to seek additional resources until you have a full understanding.

Timing of release of funds: Often investors will tie the release of funds to the achievement of certain milestones. For example, the entrepreneur might receive the first $150,000 of a $400,000 Series A round upon signing of the deal.

The next $100,000 may be released after the completion of a prototype, and the final $150,000 released when customer trials are signed. If the milestones are met by the agreed upon dates, the investors are obligated to invest. When milestones aren't met, there will be consequences. Equity capital is never free.

Anti-dilution terms: In Seed, Startup, and Early Stage companies, the value of the company often goes down before it goes up. Sometimes investors will create terms to protect their percentage of ownership and the price of their original shares when future investment occurs in case subsequent investors force a lower valuation than the previous investors. That protection often comes at the expense of the common shares which are typically founders' shares.

Liquidation preferences and redemption rights: These
two provisions can affect the potential sale of the company.

Investors may negotiate to be paid a pre-determined amount
when the company is sold, liquidated, or dissolved before
the entrepreneur or common shareholders receive anything.
If the company has a favorable exit, this may not be such an
issue. However, overly aggressive liquidation preferences
can create a high hurdle for the sales price of the company.
Investors may also negotiate the right to convert their stock
into cash plus accrued dividends at a future specified
date, usually at least five years out. If the company under
performs, or if founders aren't ready to exit, redemption
rights can force the sale of a company.

Voting rights: There will always be decisions that require
a shareholders' vote. Two-thirds approval is typical; higher
percentages increase the opportunity for one investor
to block a decision. This can work for and against the
entrepreneur, depending on the circumstances. It's wise to
structure things so that blocking a decision takes at least
two votes.

Board of directors: You will never raise angel or venture capital without adding at least one, often, two investors to your board. You want individuals who will actively contribute to your company. Remember during negotiations, the board can hire and fire management, so you want to have a good relationship with these individuals.

There is an annotated example of a term sheet in the Appendix for you to use as a learning tool. We also list term sheet sources.

Your investors and attorney may think you understand more about valuation and term sheets than you actually do. This is not the time to bluff or pretend. If there is something you don't understand, ask. And keep asking until you understand every word and line.

CONCLUSION

If a new company follows the hockey-stick trajectory that many entrepreneurs optimistically predict, valuation and terms don't become an issue. Everyone makes money.

But how many Seed and Startup State companies achieve hockey stick growth? Not many, if any. Most seed and start-up companies progress in fits and starts. They overcome hurdles to move ahead, only to encounter surprises and setbacks that cause them to have to regroup and change course. Milestones take more time and money to achieve. This is normal. Investors expect it, and you should, too.

That's why entrepreneurs who insist on valuations that are too high will be subjected to more onerous terms. They compromise future working relationships with potential investors, risk alienating board members, and may even price their company right out of the equity capital game.

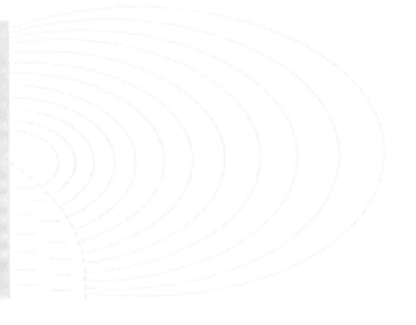

KEY POINTS

The demand for capital greatly exceeds the supply.

The initial valuation process reflects the first time that investment capital is received.

Valuation affects how much of the company the founder must give up in return for much-needed capital; the investors' ROI, and the company's ability to raise additional capital in future rounds.

A common pitfall that many Seed, Startup, and Early Stage entrepreneurs make is over-valuing their companies. This drives investors away.

For seed stage companies, expect a pre-money valuation of between $500,000 and $3 million.

The valuation process has its own methods and vocabulary. Engage an experienced entrepreneur, an attorney, or CPA to help you become more knowledgeable.

Make creating a collaborative, trusting relationship between entrepreneur and investors a goal of the valuation process.

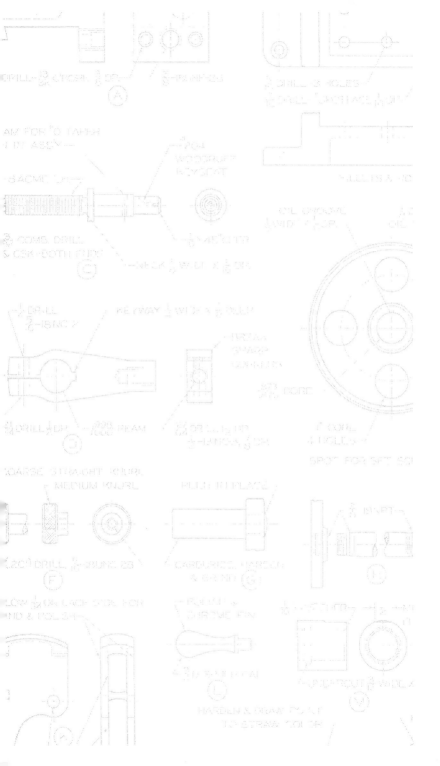

"A man only learns two ways, one by reading, and the other by association with smarter people."

– Will Rogers

THE RELATIONSHIPS

7

On many days, being the founder and CEO of a company is a solitary job. You can discuss a lot about business with your management team. You certainly want their perspectives and input, but you can't tell them everything.

This is especially true when the company is facing very tough trade-offs, considering strategic alliances with service providers and suppliers, making decisions about compensation, establishing employment policies, or dealing with sensitive personnel matters.

It is important to build relationships beyond your company with people you know you can trust. Your relationships may be informal with former professors, advisors, and/or mentors.

They may come about through your participation in community organizations, such as the Chamber of Commerce and other economic development groups. They may be formalized through a Board of Advisors or prescribed by laws governing Board of Directors.

The relationship you have with your board of directors is arguably one of the most important relationships that an entrepreneur develops as he or she is building a company. Yet many entrepreneurs don't have any experience working with boards. They often don't understand a board's role, legal obligations, or capacity to help the company gain traction and grow.

This chapter begins with purposeful networking and then covers board of advisors. However, our primary focus is to provide ideas to help you create the right board of directors for your company and then develop the processes and tools to work smoothly and effectively together to grow your company.

PURPOSEFUL NETWORKING FOR CONTACTS AND KEY HIRES

Opportunities for networking come along every day, from organized events to casual encounters. In fact, there are so many ways to network that you could spend all your time doing that instead of testing your product, writing your business plan, practicing your business plan presentation, or talking to potential customers. And this is the point.

Building contacts and relationships within the entrepreneurial ecosystem is critical to the success of new companies. Time management is more critical. Be a community partner. Don't wait until you need information or help, and especially don't wait until you begin fund raising, to get know other business people and entrepreneurs.

When you attend a networking event, introduce yourself to at least three people you haven't met before. Ask them what they do and why they are there. Exchange business cards.

This is the perfect time to practice your elevator pitch, but be sensitive and do not dominate the conversation. You are trying to establish contacts and relationships for the future, not prove that you are entrepreneur of the year.

If a person is interesting, either as a human or as a business contact, follow up your initial meeting with an email, phone call, or invitation to coffee. Set a weekly goal of two to four of these follow up activities. Create a system (beyond your iPhone) for recording information about the people you meet.

You will be surprised at how many people are interested in and willing to help entrepreneurs. You may find a mentor or two. When it comes time to raise money, identify a critical hire, or when you need a personal reference with a bank, you can turn to these people for help and advice.

Many providers recognize the financial limitations that entrepreneurs face. They may offer pro bono services or reduced rates to entrepreneurs they know and trust, recognizing that as new companies succeed, they can become long-term, profitable clients.

For example, you, like almost every entrepreneur we have met, will need the help of a well-qualified chief financial officer (CFO) long before you can afford to pay for this skill full time. If you don't know exactly what a CFO does, use your contacts to meet and talk with one to find out.

While your company is still in the Proof-of-Concept Stage, begin looking for an individual with financial skills who would be willing to work with your company part-time or on a consulting basis. This is not the time to rely on a family member, friend, or intern who has an accounting degree or a non-financial professional with the company to manage the books.

An additional resource is a business incubator or economic development organization in your area. Get to know the people there. Business incubators are typically staffed by professionals who understand the challenges faced by an entrepreneur. Not only do incubators offer shared space at very reasonable rates, they are staffed by professionals who understand the world of the entrepreneur. Incubators also provide a feeling of community with other entrepreneurs.

BOARD OF ADVISORS

While you are in the Proof of Concept or early Seed Stage, before your company has outside investors, you may choose to operate with a board of advisors.

A board of advisors is a small group of people you know and trust who have knowledge and experience that is relevant to you your business. They might be individuals in the market you are seeking to serve. They may have technical, financial, or human relations expertise. They may be entrepreneurs themselves who have successfully started and exited companies or former mentors or professors.

Many entrepreneurs find this an effective way to begin to learn how to operate with a Board and a way to identify and "road test" potential future directors.

Having an advisory board, especially if one or more of the participants are well-known and respected in the industry or market you are trying to serve adds instant credibility. This is especially true for companies in technology, medical devices, or life sciences.

Unlike boards of directors, boards of advisors do not carry legal or fiduciary obligations. You can organize and staff an advisory board in the way that is most helpful to you and your business goals.

Typical advisory boards have three or four members who have the time to serve. Although they are often more than willing, it's usually not the best idea in the world to create a board of advisors made up of friends and family members. The same goes for employees. In addition, be sure to avoid any conflicts of interest.

Meet with your advisory board periodically with a well-defined agenda. Consider compensating them for their preparation time and participation in board meetings. Individuals of this caliber are in high demand. They have other jobs and commitments.

Certainly many advisors feel a psychic reward in helping a young company gain its legs, but financial compensation can keep the relationship going when the advisor's interest declines or other demands take priority.

BUILDING A BOARD OF DIRECTORS

Corporations are required to have a board of directors elected by the stockholders. Once you secure outside funding, term documents will require the company to have a board of directors.

BOARD RESPONSIBILITIES

Boards of directors have legal responsibility in the form of fiduciary duties which include duty of care and duty of loyalty. They are obligated to protect and grow the corporation, always act in the corporation's best interests, to hold to the company's mission, and never engage in any conflict of interest or use any information obtained for personal gain.

Boards of directors don't have the power to sign contracts or commit the corporation legally, but the board does elect the corporate officers (including you) who are responsible for running the business day to day.

An effective board aligns financial and strategic expectations of the company within the board and with the CEO. The board and the CEO understand and agree with the expectations of the other. Most of the board's activities should be directed toward building the company.

The goal is to increase the value of the business and support the activities that will lead to achieving the agreed upon milestones in the fastest and most efficient way possible.

Although angel investors and venture capitalists will almost always require one or two seats on the board as a condition of funding, as CEO, you can influence the make-up of the rest of your board. Start by imagining the kind of talent you would like to have accessible to you. Could your company use more financial expertise? Marketing savvy? Experience in dealing with the Department of Defense, the FDA, or in a particular market?

Use your full board when raising capital. They can help when talking to angel investors or venture capitalists. They can be adept at negotiating valuation and board sets.

It is heartbreaking to see a CEO not in lockstep with the board on fund raising. We've seen companies struggle and even fail when the CEO insists on keeping the board at arm's length.

Boards accomplish things when the members either have or can build good working relationships. Look for people who are collaborative with strong personal networks and problem-solving experiences. Prior board experience is beneficial. Find people with strong respect for customers and for what it takes to build a company from scratch. You want at least one person on your board who understands that a CEO's job can be the loneliest job in the world.

BOARD SIZE

There is no restriction on the maximum number of board members. There are sometimes minimums, which may vary by state. For small companies, five (including the CEO) is a good number to start. As your company grows, you may choose to expand your board to seven seats. Have an odd number of board members to prevent deadlock and ties.

A company needs only as many members as it takes to provide the expertise you need. As with advisors, forget about family members, friends, or employees. You need expertise on your board; you don't need a rock star. Don't invite a big name, just for the sake of the name. You want directors who have time to devote to your company.

Build and prioritize a list of candidates. Use your executive summary and business plan as the basis for your discussions with these people. Share your vision and plans for the company.

Arrange contact with existing board members or investors. Explore whether the candidate has the time and geographic availability to serve. The very process of speaking to people about serving on your board may reveal additional candidates.

 You don't have to reinvent the wheel. Study the boards of other companies in your industry. Talk with attorneys, CPA, bankers, and consultants. Look to individuals who have experience in your industry.

A smooth working board of directors will make your company stronger. A weak board will tie your hands. But, don't forget. Your actions as CEO influence board behavior as well.

RULES FOR THE BOARD
Create a working environment that allows the board to serve your company at each stage of the Entrepreneurial Path.

It is helpful to prepare a written document, sometimes called Delegation of Authority, which defines the CEO's and Board's roles. The document will state which CEO decisions require board approval, including dollar limits. Establish term limits up front before you fill out your board. Some term limits may be tied to investors' terms, but the company can set non-investor term limits, and you should.

As the company progresses from Seed to Startup to early Growth and the role of the board changes, the definition of CEO and board roles may need to be modified, too.

Every board needs a chairperson. This can be the CEO, but it doesn't have to be. The board chairperson and the CEO will jointly develop the agenda for board meetings.

BOARD MEETINGS

With Seed to early Growth Stage companies, monthly board meetings are common. It is up to the CEO to set the format and tone to make the meetings effective and productive. Begin by creating clear guidelines for board meetings. Ask other entrepreneurs or trusted advisors what they have seen work. Schedule the calendar a full year in advance and hold the dates sacred.

Have in-person meetings if at all possible. Online meetings are a great time and money saver, but there is no substitute for building a terrific working relationship face to face.

It is wise to discuss every topic with every board member before the meeting. This saves meeting time, and gives you the opportunity to answer questions, hear objections and suggestions, and revise your action plans and recommendations based on what you learn.

Follow the good practices you learned when you were writing your business plan. Summarize your update to the board and provide the goals for the meeting on the first page of the board materials you send out. At the start of each meeting, summarize the company's overall goals, strategy, and tactics.

Don't assume that your board members will remember details from meeting to meeting—especially the numbers. However, they all know how to read financial statements so put the financials in the board material, and limit the financials in your board presentation to one summary slide.

When possible, include your management team in board meetings. They will benefit from direct interaction with the board, and the board will get to know them and appreciate their competency. These exchanges also help your team be more individually accountable to the board.

You can have closed sessions before or after the meeting. The format for board meetings often includes ending with an executive session without management attendance. After that, you and your board chair should meet to discuss the results of the meeting and next steps.

These days, comfortable dress is often appropriate, but that doesn't mean that your board presentation or approach to board meetings should be casual. Stand up and take control of the meeting. It's yours. Be a tad on the formal side.

Don't ever be defensive with your board. Effective board members don't want to run your company or take over your job. They want to use their experience and contacts to help you solve problems, meet milestones, and achieve the objectives you mutually hold.

BOARD COMMUNICATIONS – WRITTEN AND OTHERWISE

Send out board materials at least forty eight hours in advance of each board or board committee meeting. The first page in the package should be a summary that includes:

- Technology development timelines
- Sales statistics, including significant contracts
- Product rollout status
- Status of major initiatives
- Changes in key customer or business partner relationships
- Significant changes in market or competition
- Financial Statements
- Legal or accounting issues
- Personnel issues – key hires, departures, anything that can impact the business plan

Establish a regular pattern of communications between formal board meetings. Call board members. Ask their advice. Keep them informed of major developments as they occur.

FOCUS ON FINANCIALS

A one page financial statement is handy for your board and to use inside the company as well. You and your board can come up with a suitable format.

Your financial one-pager will include a balance sheet, profit and loss, and cash flows, with the major emphasis on cash. Include data from previous reporting periods.

Be sure to notate slippage in schedules, money, contacts, hiring, etc. from board meeting to board meeting.

Represent the key spending areas and your burn rate. If your business has significant investments in equipment, include that. Be sure to report bookings or cancellation of contracts, headcount by department, and updates on significant events impacting the current summary over the last one.

BOARD MINUTES

Board meeting minutes are the official record of what transpired during each board meeting. They should be reviewed for accuracy and approved by each board member and then filed in a safe place with other permanent records. Corrections or additions to the minutes should be raised at the next board meeting.

Minutes can be used as evidence in legal proceedings. It is advisable to sit down with a trusted advisor to understand the level of detail appropriate for board minutes. Although board minutes for private companies are not public documents, upon sale or acquisition of the company or other "exit" scenarios, the board minutes will be reviewed in detail as part of due diligence.

It is always good to consult your attorney for help establishing these parameters at the beginning of the company's life. As the company grows, you will want to consider a legal secretary for the board.

Board Minutes – the minimum

- *Name of the organization*
- *Location, date, and time of meeting*
- *Board members in attendance, excused and absent*
- *Other attendees*
- *Existence of a quorum*
- *Description of agenda item and board action*

As your company progresses from Proof-of-Concept to the Growth Stage and you make key new hires or reward existing employees, you will be coming to your board (or the compensation committee of the board) for approval of grants of equity. Develop a standard format for making these requests that includes the most current capitalization table, even if it hasn't changed.

Put each grant and each planned recipient in context compared to previously awarded grants. Be prepared to discuss the contribution and performance of anyone on the table. Your board may ask.

Here's an example of how to present the information to your board:

NAME	POSITION	#OF SHARES	PERECNT OWNERSHIP	#EXISTING SHARES/% VESTED	RANGE

By following a standard procedure, you teach your board what to expect, make the information readily available, and create a discipline for yourself and your company that will result in a smooth timely granting of shares. This enhances your credibility with your employees and your board.

BOARD COMPENSATION AND DIRECTORS' INSURANCE

If you want an active engaged board, compensate them. Cash compensation for board service in an early company is not desirable. Options align the board with management. It is common to award one-time options in the range of .25 to 1 percent of the outstanding company stock with the options vesting annually over two to five years.

Make it clear up front how the vesting will work if the member leaves the board. Investors (angels and venture capitalists) serve on the board as dictated by their investment. They do not receive additional equity or compensation.

Always reimburse board members for reasonable and actual expenses. Reasonable means expenses that conform to the company's typical practices. Everyone, board members included, must be mindful of cash in early companies, and if they aren't, you might have the wrong board member.

Ensure that the charter of your company contains a specific clause that limits directors' liability and that corporate documents provide indemnification protection so that if a claim is made, the director is reimbursed for costs and possible judgments. Then expect to provide directors and officers liability insurance (D&O) so that board members and their assets can be protected.

Board actions are measured against the legal standard of reasonable care. The board demonstrates performance of the duty of care with minutes, notes, expert opinions, and advice from independent consultants. This is especially true when discussions and decisions have to do with selling the company.

CONCLUSION

Building contacts and relationships within the entrepreneurial ecosystem is critical to the success of new companies.

Close and trusting relationships with individuals who bring a different perspective will help you create a better, stronger company and will benefit you personally. Network with purpose.

When it comes time to raise money, identify a critical hire, or when you need a personal reference with a bank, you can turn to these people for help and advice.

An entrepreneur's relationship with the board of directors can be one of the most beneficial tools a new company has to gain traction and grow. Equity investors will require one or two board seats as part of the terms of the deal. Often these individuals will be persons involved in due diligence and/or the negotiation of valuation. Remember this, and don't burn your bridges.

Boards of directors are obligated to protect and grow the corporation, always act in the corporation's best interests, to hold to the company's mission, and never engage in any conflict of interest or use any information obtained for personal gain.

KEY POINTS

Build purposeful relationships within the business, academic, and entrepreneurial communities from day one.

Don't wait until you need it to ask for help and advice.

Invest time and thoughtful preparation in building a board of directors.

Be totally professional and respectful in every interaction with your board, from memos to formal board meetings.

Your board is your ally. Ask for their help, and then take it.

Effective CEOs work closely and well with their Boards.

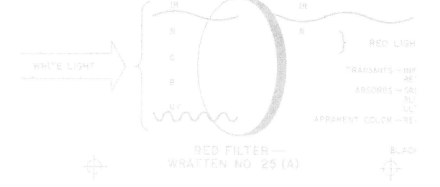

WHITE LIGHT

IR
R
O
B
UV

RED FILTER —
WRATTEN NO. 25 (A)

IR
R

RED LIGHT

TRANSMITS — INF
RE

ABSORBS — GRE
BL
UL

APPARENT COLOR — RE

BLACK

"All Wrigley had was an idea. He was the first man to discover that American jaws must wag. So why not give them something to wag against?"

– *Will Rogers*

THE EXIT

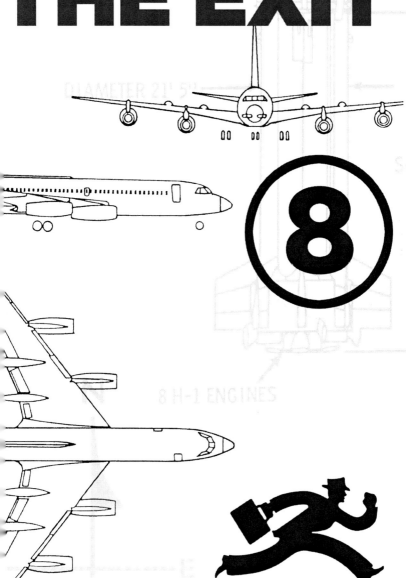

8

You've reached the last chapter of this handbook. This is the place we talk about the rewards of all your hard work.

You've created your business plan, successfully attracted the appropriate investors at each stage of growth, and managed cash more tightly than Scrooge. You can deliver your Elevator and Business Plan pitch in your sleep.

You've built strong relationships with your board of directors and with business leaders in your community. You have solid contracts with customers who are more than satisfied with your products.

You feel like you could teach a class on market development and risk management. You've learned how to hire, motivate, and reward talented people. Your business is better than profitable, it is cash flow positive. You are paying yourself a decent salary—maybe for the first time since you became an entrepreneur.

You've done what you told your investors you would do. You've reached the Growth Stage of the Entrepreneurial Path.

What's next?

YOUR EXIT STRATEGY

What were your expectations when you set out to build a company? Did you plan to run it for the next 20 or 30 years? Or did you expect to go off and do something else?

From the moment you set your entrepreneurial toes on the starting line, answering these questions need to be part of your strategy. Once you know what you want for yourself, that will define what you want for your company.

You may or may not be able to achieve your desire, but you will be able to communicate it honestly and openly to your employees and potential investors and work together to build a strategy to achieve it.

FACTOID

Mergerstat database shows the median price of private company acquisitions is under $25 million when the price is disclosed.

If your personal objective in building your company doesn't match your investors' or your key employees, then you will either have to change your goal or establish different relationships.

If this turns out to be the case, the sooner you and they recognize this, the better. There is no margin in a successful entrepreneurial company for misaligned goals.

So as the entrepreneur-founder of a company that successfully reaches the Growth Stage, what are the possible choices that may be available to you?

- Continue as owner and CEO
- Sell your company to a larger company and stay involved in some capacity
- Recapitalize the business and partially or fully cash out
- Get invited out

Your board of directors, your investors, and likely your spouse or significant other will all have input to your decision.

You may be about to discover what many entrepreneurs already know. Building a business can be more fun than selling it.

CONSIDERING EXIT SCENARIOS

When your company reaches the Growth Stage, you take a breath and enjoy the success for a little while, but eventually you are going to need more capital.

To capture more market share, companies in the Growth Stage invest in product development to create new lines or in business development to reach new markets. Maybe you even have a requirement to invest in bricks and mortar to expand manufacturing.

What are your options for raising that money, and how do they match up with your personal goals?

To continue on as owner and CEO, you will need the support of your board to:

- **Raise more private equity capital** – possible, though not likely as the investors you have are probably more than ready to get their money out

or

- **IPO** – even less likely. Between 2007 and 2010, there were fewer than 120 total IPOs in the U.S.

- **To sell your company to a larger company,**
  you will need:
  A funded acquisition strategy agreed upon by your board of directors and supported by key employees and all investors

and

A buyer

- **To cash out,** you will need one of these:
  An acquistion
  An IPO
  An investor who wants to purchase your shares

- **To get invited out**, one or more of these will probably accomplish your goal:

Fail to grow with the company

Fail to make the transition from entrepreneur to CEO

Mislead your investors and employees about your true goals

Create an adversarial relationship with your board

Ignore your investors' desires regarding timing and ROI

Make some other really big mistake

 Big IPOs are rare. Big merger and acquisition transactions are infrequent. This is a good era for entrepreneurs because it costs less than ever to start a technology company. Product development in fields like software can be faster than ever before. Big companies have cash reserves and would rather buy than build innovation.

ACQUISITION DESERVES SERIOUS CONSIDERATION

In case you haven't noticed, we don't spend much time in this handbook talking about IPOs. That's because they aren't an option for most entrepreneurs. These days, only the very best companies, and very few of those, have a shot at an IPO.

An acquisition on the other hand, is a very good option. Odds are, your investors will point you in this direction. Listen to them. They understand the entrepreneurial path much better than you.

Acquisition has been a predictable part of the strategy in life sciences for a very long time. Now it's becoming the norm in other high growth industries as well with big names like

Microsoft, Google, Apple, and IBM acquiring small companies
with interesting technologies, applications, or market traction.

You don't hear a lot about these deals, but they are
happening. Every day. Big companies spend $10 to
$30 million on companies with plans to grow them into
business units of $100 million or more. Big companies
know that they aren't good at innovation. They know that
small companies are.

**Read these to become more knowledgeable
about exits and to gain an understanding of
angel and VC perspectives.**

Early Exits, by Basil Peters

Berkonomics and Extending the Runway
by Dave Berkus

Strategic Entrepreneurism by Jon Fisher

*Invest to Exit; The Ultimate Deal 2;
Ultimate Exits; and Ultimate Exits
Workbook* by Dr. Tom McKaskill

The trend toward acquisition creates an opportunity for entrepreneurs to make an outstanding return in a relatively brief timeframe. Remember our earlier example, $10 million in 4 percent tax free bonds generates $300,000 per year.

IDENTIFY STRATEGIC BUYERS; EXPRESS YOUR FIRM'S VALUE ADD

The secret to a successful acquisition is to find a strategic buyer. As you are growing your company, consider partners, key suppliers, and even competitors. Create a "shopping" list of what you would want in a buyer for your firm. Create another list of the value your company could deliver to such a buyer.

Engage your investors and board. Work with them to build appropriate momentum. Use the same approach thinking about potential buyers as you did when you were first analyzing the markets for your company. Use the same tools you used in your valuation process to hunt out industry comparables.

Think of ways to make your company the first choice of a bigger player in your industry. Cultivate and showcase customers that are attractive to them. Think about your business as a product. What is the best way to package it?

Build your products so that they integrate with potential buyers' solutions. Hire people your potential buyer would want to hire. Understand how your company solves customer problems that an acquirer would want to solve.

EXITING THE EXIT

Most of the successful entrepreneurs we know start multiple companies. Some of these are more successful than others. Just remember that once you've navigated a successful exit and have all your learned experience and that $3 to $10 million in the bank, you are in the ideal place to hatch your next big idea.

CONCLUSION

An entrepreneur has to think with two minds. On one hand, your goal is to found a company that can gain traction and grow. On the other hand, you have to think about the appropriate exit for your investors and yourself.

There is no one right answer; the most important thing is to be honest and realistic about your objectives. Your job is to keep your company, investor, board, and personal objectives aligned. That can be a real balancing act, even for the most experienced entrepreneur.

KEY POINTS

Develop exit scenarios early in the company's life.

Be honest and open with your investors and board.

Your company will only be successful if your interests are aligned.

This may mean that you leave and/or sell the company before you are ready.

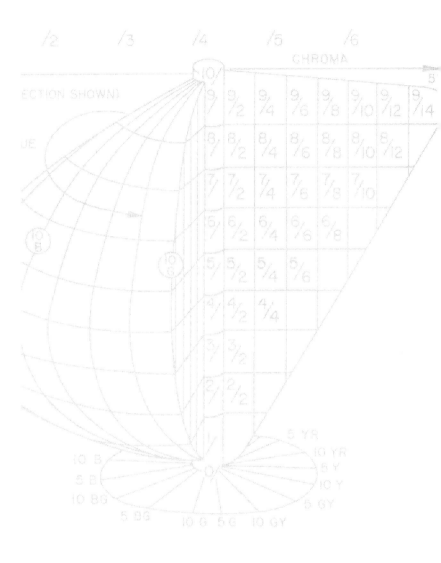

Glossary

Accredited Investor: For an individual to be considered an accredited investor, he or she must have a net worth of at least one million US dollars excluding the value of their primary residence or have made at least $200,000 each year for the last two years ($300,000 with his or her spouse if married) and have the expectation to make the same amount the current year.

Acquisition: This is when another company buys your company. You and your investors divide the proceeds according to your percent of ownership. The acquiring company views your business as advantageous to their own growth strategy.

Advanced Technologies: These are state-of-the-art proprietary products, processes, materials, designs, and/or know-how.

Advisory Board: These are individuals you know and trust who can assist you in the stages of the Entrepreneurial Path before a Board of Directors is needed. Working with an advisory board can be an effective way to learn to operate with a formal board.

Angel Investor: An angel investor is a wealthy individual who meets the criteria of accredited investor and provides capital for a startup business in return for ownership shares in the business or convertible debt. Angels often organize into angel groups or angel networks to share deal flow, due diligence on potential investment companies, and to pool their investment capital.

Anti-dilution Terms: In Seed, Startup, and Early Stage companies, the value of the company often goes down before it goes up. Investors will create terms to protect their percentage of ownership and the price of their original shares when future investment occurs in case subsequent investors force a lower valuation than the previous investors. That protection often comes at the expense of the common shares.

Banks: Local banks, and to some extent national ones, may be a source of lines of credit, traditional borrowing, or convertible debt.

Big Ideas: These are the kind of ideas that entrepreneurs base companies on. See Big Problems and Big Markets.

Big Markets: A Big Market is enough potential customers who would be willing to pay for your company's product or service to create a profitable self-sustaining business. To grow your company along the Entrepreneurial Path, your Big Idea must solve a Big Problem for a Big Market.

Big Problems: A Big Problem is what all successful companies solve for their markets. Entrepreneurs who are founding high growth companies must understand the problem that their product or service solves.

Board of Directors: Corporations have a board of directors elected by the stockholders. Boards of directors have legal responsibility in the form of fiduciary duties which include duty of care and duty of loyalty. They are obligated to protect and grow the corporation, always act in the corporation's best interests, to hold to the company's mission, and never engage in any conflict of interest or use any information obtained for personal gain.

Bootstrap: Bootstrapping requires entrepreneurs to use imagination, know-how, and hard work to pay as they go through revenue without raising equity capital.

Breakeven: When a company can pay its expenses from its revenues.

Business: A business is a commercial enterprise that produces a product or service to be sold to a specific market.

Business Pitch: A succinct presentation made by the entrepreneur that represents their business opportunity.

Business Plan: A detailed process of how an entrepreneur plans to bring a product to market.

Capital: See equity capital.

Capital Requirements: The amount of funds needed to progress to the next stage of the Entrepreneurial Path.

Capitalization Table (CAP table): A CAP table is a document that shows who owns what percentage of the company and what they paid for their share.

Chief Executive Officer (CEO): The highest ranking executive in a company. The CEO's main responsibilities include developing and implementing high-level strategies, making major corporate decisions, managing the overall operations and resources of a company, and acting as the main point of communication between the board of directors and the corporate operations.

Chief Financial Officer (CFO): The senior manager who is responsible for overseeing the financial activities of the entire company. This includes signing checks, monitoring cash flow, overseeing audits, and financial planning.

Convertible Debt: Some investors and banks will offer capital under terms of convertible debt. In these borrowing arrangements, the lender has the option to convert the debt into shares of equity at a specified point in time.

Dilution: A reduction in earnings per share of common stock that occurs through the issuance of additional shares or the conversion of convertible securities.

Directors and Officers Insurance (D&O): D&O insurance is liability insurance that provides financial protection to the directors and officers of your company in the event they are sued in conjunction with the performance of their duties while acting in their capacity as directors and officers for the organization.

Down Round: A round of financing where investors purchase stock from a company at a lower valuation than the valuation placed upon the company by earlier investors.

Dry Powder: Savvy investors often hold back a portion of investment capital in anticipation of unexpected events.

Early Stage: The stage on the Entrepreneurial Path where beta testing has begun and the company may be approaching breakeven with respect to expense and revenue.

Elevator Pitch: A 45-second presentation of the basics, long enough to share with someone on an elevator ride.

Entrepreneur's Risk Assessment: This is a thought-starter for evaluating the activities that relate to the product or service you plan to provide, the market your product will serve, and the viability of the business you want to build.

Entrepreneurs: Entrepreneurs play a key role in any economy. These are the people who have the skills and initiative necessary to take good new ideas to market and make the right decisions to make the companies they found profitable. The reward for the risks taken is the potential economic profits the entrepreneur could earn.

Entrepreneurial Path: A structured process entrepreneurs follow to take their Big Idea from Proof-of-Concept to Growth.

Equity Capital: Fund provided by investors in return for shares of the company. These funds are used to pay for expansion and growth and the company moves along the Entrepreneurial Path.

Equity Investment: Investments made in return for a percentage ownership in the company, which usually takes the form of common or preferred shares of stock.

Execution: This means carrying out the company's business plan; execution is often discussed in terms of risk.

Exit: At some point, either when your company reaches the Growth Stage of the Entrepreneurial Path or before, your investors will want to exit from your business to cash out their investment and realize their gains.

Exit Strategy: Every smart entrepreneur anticipates that there will be an exit event at some point. Start building your strategy from day one. Make sure your goals and interests and those of your investors are aligned.

Finance: This means the capital and cash flow required to achieve the milestones that lead to a high growth company's success.

Fire Sale: This is when the company has reached the point where it cannot survive on its own revenues and investors are no longer willing to provide more capital. This is not a good way to exit a business.

First Round, Second Round: This ordinal nomenclature is used to describe most venture rounds. Companies will casually call their rounds first, second, third, etc. even though the legal term for the transaction as stated in closing documents and amendments to the documents of incorporation may refer to them as Series A preferred, Series B common, etc.

Founders, Friends, and Family: You will be your first investor. After that, family, friends, and acquaintances will often invest very early in the company's lifecycle as their trust and interest is in the individual than in the possibility of significant monetary returns.

Grant: Grants come from businesses, foundations, and public and private sector organizations. Some grants require the entrepreneur to come up with matching funds from other sources. Unlike loans or equity capital from investors, grants do not have to be repaid.

Growth Stage: The stage on the Entrepreneurial Path when the company is producing revenue and is profitable.

High Growth Company: This is a company whose revenue growth profile or potential exit profile is much larger and faster than most companies. These types of companies offer investors large returns on their investments.

Hockey Stick: A pattern of growth that starts out level and flat like the blade of a hockey stick and then at some point gains momentum and curves upward with nearly vertical growth, resembling the handle of the stick. Many entrepreneurs forecast hockey stick growth. Few companies actually achieve it.

Initial Public Offering (IPO): The first sale of stock by a private company to the public. IPOs are often issued by smaller, younger companies seeking the capital to expand, but can also be done by large privately owned companies looking to become publicly traded. IPOs are very uncommon.

Key Employees: Those individuals a high growth business needs to achieve its milestones and reach profitability. Typical key skills are marketing, finance, and engineering.

Later Stage to Maturity: This is the stage on the Entrepreneurial Path when equity capital and traditional funds support expansion, growth, and potentially strategic acquisitions to enter new markets.

Liquidation Preferences and Redemption Rights: Investors may negotiate to be paid a pre-determined amount when the company is sold, liquidated, or dissolved before the entrepreneur or common shareholders receive anything. If the company has a favorable exit, this may not be such an issue.

Liquidity: An asset's ability to be sold without causing a significant movement in the price and with minimum loss of value. Liquidity also refers both to a business's ability to meet its payment obligations.

Market: This refers to a commercial activity where goods and services are sold.

Market Research: Learning about the market for your product or services. Market research can be as simple and low cost as interviewing potential customers or performing Internet searches on competitors. It can be as costly as purchasing full-blown market information.

Mezzanine: A mezzanine equity investment round is generally characterized as the last venture round prior to an IPO.

Milestone: Critical events that must happen for a company to progress on the Entrepreneurial Path. Typically funding is matched to the achievement of certain milestones.

Net Present Value (NPV): The difference between the present value of cash inflows and the present value of cash outflows. NPV is used in capital budgeting to analyze the profitability of an investment or project. Return on Investment (ROI): A performance measure used to evaluate the efficiency of an investment or to compare the efficiency of a number of different investments. The return on investment formula: ROI = (gain from investment – cost of investment) ÷ cost of investment.

Payout: Investors' and founders' returns when a company is sold.

Personal Resources: This refers to the assets that an entrepreneur has to invest in the company he or she is founding—cash, home, bank accounts, equities, or retirement accounts.

Portfolio: A grouping of companies in which angel investors or venture capitalists have invested equity capital. These investors tend to invest in multiple deals to create a diversified portfolio that helps balance their risk.

Post-Money: The value of a company after external financing alternatives is added to its balance sheet, for example the value of a company after angel investors invest.

Pre-Money: The value of a company before external financing is added to its balance sheet, for example, the value of a company before angel investors invest.

Product: A tangible object, technology, or service offered for sale.

Profitability: When the company has money remaining after accounting for all the expenses. Consistently earning profit is every company's goal. If a company doesn't achieve profitability, it cannot survive.

Proof-of-Concept Stage: The stage on the Entrepreneurial Path where the product and business concept is developed.

Purposeful Networking: Establishing contacts and relationships from the early days of starting your company. The goal is to build long-term mutually beneficial relationships with the entrepreneurial community, other business leaders, and the appropriate public sector and academic entities.

Seed Stage: The stage on the Entrepreneurial Path when the company has a product or service at a very early stage of development but probably not fully operational.

Series A: Typically the first equity capital that a company receives, often from angel investors, rarely from venture capitalists. The funds are used for the introduction of a working product prototype or pilot to the market to verify that the economics of the business plan are sustainable.

Series B, C, etc.: Equity rounds that occur after the initial round, commonly referred to as second round or Series B and so on. These later stage rounds are typically used to fund product and market development.

Small Business: The U.S. Small Business Administration (SBA) defines a small business as having fewer than 500 employees for manufacturing businesses and less than $7 million in annual receipts for most nonmanufacturing businesses.

Small Business Innovation Research Program (SBIR): This competitive award program is administered by the U.S. Small Business Administration (SBA) Office of Technology to ensure that the nation's small, high-tech, innovative businesses are a significant part of the federal government's research and development efforts. Eleven federal departments participate in the SBIR program.

Small Business Technology Transfer Program (STTR): This competitive award program is administered by the U.S. Small Business Administration (SBA) Office of Technology. In this competitive program the SBA ensures that the nation's small, high-tech, innovative businesses are a significant part of the federal government's research and development efforts. Five federal departments participate in the STTR program.

Small Businesses Administration (SBA): The U.S. Small Business Administration is an independent agency of the federal government to aid, counsel, assist and protect the interests of small business concerns, to preserve free competitive enterprise and to maintain and strengthen the overall economy of our nation.

Sources of capital: Funding resources the company requires while progressing along the Entrepreneurial Path. Some are more likely than others, and they vary from stage to stage. Sources may include friends, family, grants, angel investors, bank loans and lines of credit, and/or venture capital.

Startup Stage: The stage on the Entrepreneurial Path when companies typically introduce a new product to the market.

Syndication: Multiple investors, which may include individual angels, angel groups, and venture capitalists, pooling their funds to provide larger investments and to diversify risk.

Term Sheet: A non-binding agreement setting forth the basic terms and conditions under which equity investors (angels or venture capitalists) will invest in your company. Term sheet may also refer to the terms of the acquisition of your company.

The Entrepreneur's Path: A handbook for high growth companies: This handbook provides the framework, tools, and process to validate the business potential of your entrepreneurial dream.

Third, Fourth, Fifth, etc. and Later Rounds: Equity rounds that fall after the second round of financing.

Timing of Release of Funds: Often investors will tie the release of funds to the achievement of certain milestones.

Tips from the Trenches: Various tidbits of wisdom from experienced entrepreneurs and investors that the reader will find throughout The Entrepreneur's Path: a handbook for high growth companies.

Valuation: The process of determining the current worth of an asset or company. There are many techniques that can be used to determine value, some are subjective and others are objective.

Valley of Death: This is the point during the Proof-of-Concept, Seed, Startup, and Early Stage when the company is spending more money than it is taking in, usually to build product and carry out market development. It is called the Valley of Death because so many companies don't make it out of this stage.

Venture Capital: Venture Capital is pooled investment capital from institutional investors and high net worth individuals. Because of the size of venture capital funds and operating costs, most venture capital funds find it more efficient to invest $3 million or more. This means they are more likely to seek out advanced technology businesses that are producing revenue.

Venture Capitalist (VC): A person who manages a venture capitalist fund. These investors are motivated by the potential returns on their investment.

Voting Rights: There will always be decisions that require a shareholders' vote. Two-thirds approval is typical; higher percentages increase the opportunity for one investor to block a decision.

Will Rogers: Vaudevillian, common sense speaker of the truth; Oklahoma's favorite son.

Resources Appendix

Business Advisory Services & Affiliates

Oklahoma Inventor's Assistance Service (IAS)
www.ias.okstate.edu
The IAS is a non-profit, state-funded service that helps Oklahoma inventors navigate the invention process from idea to the marketplace through education, information, and referrals.

Oklahoma Small Business Development Center (OSBDC)
www.osbdc.org
OSBDC's mission is to ensure that all Oklahomans have access to professional and confidential business counseling, educational workshops, and continuing support throughout their business ventures.

Oklahoma Department of Commerce
www.OKStartup.com
OKStartup.com is the Oklahoma Department of Commerce's one-stop resource for entrepreneurial assistance. You can sort out business licensing issues, register your business, find service providers, explore financing options, and more.

Research Wizard
www.researchwizard.org
Research Wizard is a unique service of the Tulsa City-County Library System that offers information that is customized to meet business needs and maximize time and profits.

Oklahoma Bioscience Association (OKBio)
www.okbio.org
OKBio is a statewide membership organization exclusively dedicated to the growth of Oklahoma's bioscience sector.

The State Chamber of Oklahoma
www.okstatechamber.com
The State Chamber of Oklahoma is a private, nonprofit, business-membership organization designed to advocate business needs at the state and federal levels.

Oklahoma Manufacturing Alliance
www.okalliance.com
The Oklahoma Manufacturing Alliance offers technical assistance and business advice, helping companies become progressively more successful through a statewide network of manufacturing extension agents and applications engineers.

Oklahoma Venture Forum (OVF)
www.ovf.org
The Oklahoma Venture Forum (OVF) is a non-profit corporation
organized to encourage economic development in Oklahoma.

The Riata Center for Entrepreneurship – Oklahoma State University
www.entrepreneurship.okstate.edu/riata
The Riata Center is dedicated to high impact entrepreneurial outreach
on Oklahoma State University's campus, in the region, around the State
of Oklahoma, and across America. The Center is intimately engaged
with the entrepreneurial community, and strongly committed to creating
unique experiential learning opportunities for students.

Center for the Creation of Economic Wealth (CCEW)
www.ccew.ou.edu
The Center for the Creation of Economic Wealth at the University of
Oklahoma offers opportunities for practical experience to promote the
entrepreneurial spirit and assist in developing Oklahoma's economy.

Technology Incubators

Oklahoma Technology & Research Park
www.oktechpark.com

Norman Economic Development Coalition
www.nedcok.com

The Innovation Center at Rogers State University
www.rsu.edu/innovation

Presbyterian Health Foundation (PHF) Research Park
www.phfresearchpark.com

State & Federal Grant Programs

Oklahoma Applied Research Support (OARS) Grant
www.ok.gov/ocast/Programs
The Oklahoma Applied Research Support program helps universities,
foundations and businesses fund cutting-edge research that will
benefit Oklahoma's economy. Managed by the Oklahoma Center for the
Advancement of Science & Technology (OCAST).

Small Business Innovative Research/Small Business Technology Transfer (SBIR/STTR)

www.ok.gov/ocast/Programs

SBIR and STTR are competitively awarded federal programs designed to stimulate technological innovation and provide opportunities for small businesses. These federal grant programs are administered by OCAST.

Oklahoma Nanotechnology Applications Project (ONAP)

www.ok.gov/ocast/Programs

ONAP in partnership with academic, commercialization and economic development resources in the state provides a mechanism to extend financial support and technical services for the application of nanotechnology in Oklahoma's manufacturing and business community. ONAP is administered by the Oklahoma State Chamber.

Oklahoma's Economic Development Generating Excellence (EDGE)

www.ok.gov/edge

The EDGE Fund supports technology related scientific research, collaborative public-private partnerships, and the commercialization of scientific discovery. In doing so, it contributes to the growing competitiveness of Oklahoma, it helps accelerate scientific innovation, and it plays a key role in improving Oklahoma's quality of life.

Oklahoma Health Research Program (OHR)

www.ok.gov/ocast/Programs

Administered by OCAST, the Oklahoma Health Research Program competitively awards seed funds for research projects related to human health to Oklahoma Universities and colleges, non-profit research foundations and commercial companies in Oklahoma.

Oklahoma Capital Resources

i2E, Inc.

www.i2E.org

i2E, Inc. is a private not-for-profit Oklahoma corporation focused on wealth creation by growing the technology-based entrepreneurial economy within our state. i2E originates and manages initiatives and programs that provide Oklahoma entrepreneurs, college students, and innovators with the knowledge, skills, and access to capital for turning innovations into enterprises.

Oklahoma Seed Capital Fund (OSCF)
www.i2E.org
Created in 2007, OSCF is a seed capital fund that provides seed and
start-up stage equity financing to small, technology-based Oklahoma
companies. OSCF looks and operates like a conventional venture fund
with the specific goal of furthering economic activity and success in
Oklahoma by bridging the funding gap between personal sources and
traditional sources of venture capital.

OCAST Technology Business Finance Program
www.i2E.org
The Oklahoma Technology Business Finance Program (TBFP), which
began as the brainchild of the Oklahoma Center for the Advancement of
Science and Technology (OCAST) and is funded by the state legislature.
This program is unusual in that it specifically late phase Proof-of-
Concept and early phase Seed Stage capital needs of high growth
businesses. It has been recognized nationally and internationally as a
model of best practices.

SeedStep Angels
www.seedstepangels.com
SeedStep Angels is a formalized group of accredited Angel Investors
comprised of successful entrepreneurs and business leaders in Oklahoma
who provide investment capital, strategic advice and mentoring to
emerging growth companies to help them achieve market leadership.
Seedstep Angels is managed by i2E, Inc.

Additional Oklahoma Sources

Davis, Tuttle Venture Partners (DTVP)
www.davistuttle.com
Davis, Tuttle Venture Partners (DTVP) is a private investment
partnership formed to provide emerging growth companies with the
necessary long-term development capital, as well as vital management
counsel and support.

MetaFund
www.metafund.org
MetaFund is a collaborative, non-profit, multi-bank-funded, community
development, private equity and venture capital firm.

Oklahoma Life Science Fund (OLFS)
www.olsfventures.com
OLSF invests in promising life science technologies where businesses and
management teams can be built. Investment decisions made by the Fund's limited
partners and OLSF will be the first professionally managed money invested.

National Resources

Angel Capital Association (ACA)
www.angelcapitalassociation.org
The Angel Capital Association is North America's professional alliance of angel groups. The association brings together many of the angel organizations in the United States and Canada to share best practices and collaboration opportunities. ACA provides excellent professional development and discounts on important services for angel investors who belong to member groups, and also serves as the public policy voice of the American angel community.

Angel Capital Education Foundation
www.angelcapitaleducation.org
The Angel Capital Education Foundation is a nonprofit organization that focuses on assembling research about angel investing, hosting events that will allow for discussion between angel groups and educating those interested in pursuing angel capital with their unique program entitled Power of Angel Investing.

Business Plan Archive
www.businessplanarchive.org
Business Plan Archive -In partnership with the Library of Congress, the Center for History and New Media, and the University of Maryland Libraries, the Archive collects and preserves business plans and related planning documents from the Birth of the Dot Com Era so that future generations will be able to learn from this episode in the history of technology and entrepreneurship.

Innovation America
www.innovationamerica.us
Innovation America's mission is to accelerate the growth of the entrepreneurial innovation economy in America.

International Economic Development Council
www.iedconline.org
The International Economic Development Council (IEDC) is a non-profit membership organization dedicated to helping economic developers do their job more effectively and raising the profile of the profession.

Kauffman Foundation
www.kauffman.org
The Ewing Marion Kauffman Foundation was established in the mid-1960s by the late entrepreneur and philanthropist Ewing Marion Kauffman. Based in Kansas City, Missouri, the Kauffman Foundation is among the 30 largest foundations in the United States with an asset base of approximately $2 billion.

Microsoft Startup Center
www.microsoft.com/smallbusiness/startup-toolkit
Microsoft Startup Center – Helps small businesses start off right with
an elaborate checklist that guides entrepreneurs through business plan
creation, branding, sales, finances and more. Offers on Microsoft products
also help to give users a business upper hand.

National Association of Women Business Owners
www.nawbo.org
NAWBO works to strengthen the wealth-creating capacity of its members
and promote economic development, create innovative and effective
changes in the business culture, build strategic alliances, coalitions and
affiliations, and transform public policy and influence opinion makers.
They offer many resources including educational activities, business
referrals and leadership training.

National Venture Capital Association
www.nvca.org
The National Venture Capital Association (NVCA), comprised of more
than 400 member firms, is the premier trade association that represents
the U.S. venture capital industry. NVCA's mission is to foster greater
understanding of the importance of venture capital to the U.S. economy,
and support entrepreneurial activity and innovation. The NVCA
represents the public policy interests of the venture capital community,
strives to maintain high professional standards, provides reliable industry
data, sponsors professional development, and facilitates interaction
among its members.

Pricewaterhouse Coopers NVCA MoneyTree report
www.pwcmoneytree.com
The MoneyTree Report is a quarterly study of venture capital
investment activity in the United States. A collaboration between
PricewaterhouseCoopers and the National Venture Capital Association
based upon data from Thomson Reuters, it is the only industry-endorsed
research of its kind. The MoneyTree Report is the definitive source
of information on emerging companies that receive financing and the
venture capital firms that provide it. The study is a staple of the financial
community, entrepreneurs, government policymakers and the business
press worldwide.

SBIR
www.sbir.gov
The U.S. Small Business Administration (SBA) Office of Technology
administers the Small Business Innovation Research (SBIR) Program.
Through this competitive program, SBA ensures that the nation's
small, high-tech, innovative businesses are a significant part of the
federal government's research and development efforts. Eleven federal

departments participate in the SBIR program. The U.S National Science Foundation administers the SBIR.GOV site on behalf of the federal government.

Small Business Administration
www.sba.gov
The U.S. Small Business Administration (SBA) was created in 1953 as an independent agency of the federal government to aid, counsel, assist and protect the interests of small business concerns, to preserve free competitive enterprise and to maintain and strengthen the overall economy of our nation.

STTR
www.sbir.gov
The U.S. Small Business Administration (SBA) Office of Technology administers the Small Business Technology Transfer (STTR) Program. Through this competitive program, SBA ensures that the nation's small, high-tech, innovative businesses are a significant part of the federal government's research and development efforts. Five departments participate in the STTR program.

The Center for Advanced Technology and Innovation
www.thecati.com
CATI serves as a technology transfer intermediary. CATI helps companies find a purpose for their unused technological assets by linking them with existing and star-up companies searching for solutions to their engineering, design and manufacturing challenges. They also serve as a source of information and inspiration for young businessmen and women looking to utilize the research and development that currently exists within U.S. industry; helping them create new businesses based on that previously unused technology.

The Public Forum Institute
www.publicforuminstitute.org
The Public Forum Institute is an independent, nonpartisan, not-for-profit organization committed to developing the most advanced and effective means of fostering public discourse. The Forum tailors projects that advance the exchange of information and ideas by combining issue expertise with advanced program development and communications skills.

State Science & Technology Institute
www.ssti.org
SSTI is a national nonprofit organization that leads, supports, and strengthens efforts to improve state and regional economies through science, technology, and innovation. SSTI offers the services that are needed to help build tech-based economies.

Term Sheet Resources

Sample TERM SHEET FOR SERIES A ROUND OF FINANCING OF COMPANY ABC

Amount of Investment: $150,000

Investor: Bounty Equity Fund

Type of Security: Series A Convertible Preferred Stock

Pre-money Valuation: $X
The fund may sometimes increase the valuation, pending certain milestones met over the course of 12 to 24 months.

Use of Proceeds and Staging of Payments:
The investment of $150,000 will be payable in 3 stages:

$50,000 at the closing of the round to be used for activities to be agreed upon usually related to product development milestones

$50,000 pending activities to be agreed upon usually related to product development milestones and sales and marketing milestones

$50,000 pending activities to be agreed upon usually related to product and marketing milestones and meeting certain financial targets

Other Terms: Formation of a Board of Directors with X members including one Board Seat for Bounty Equity Fund .

Dividends: The Company will not pay dividends on its shares of Common Stock or any other stock which is junior to the Series A Preferred Stock unless a like dividend is paid on all shares of Series A Preferred Stock on a pro rata "as converted" basis.

Conversion: Each share of Series A Preferred Stock shall be convertible, at any time, at the option of the holder, into shares of Common Stock, at an initial conversion ratio of one share of Common Stock for each share of Series A Preferred Stock.

Anti-dilution: The terms of the Series A Preferred Stock will contain standard "weighted average" anti-dilution protection with respect to the issuance by the Company of equity securities at a price per share less than the applicable conversion price then in effect, subject to standard and customary exceptions. The conversion rate of the Series A Preferred Stock into common stock will be adjusted appropriately to account for any stock splits, recapitalizations, mergers, combinations and asset sales, stock dividends, and similar events.

Voting Rights: On all matters submitted for stockholder approval, each share of Series A Preferred Stock shall be entitled to such number of votes as is equal to the number of shares of Common Stock into which such shares are convertible. In addition, the Company shall not, without the prior consent of the holders of at least a majority of the then issued and outstanding Series A Preferred Stock, voting as a separate class:

- issue or create any series or class of securities with rights superior to or on a parity with the Series A Preferred Stock or increase the rights or preferences of any series or class having rights or preferences that are junior to the Series A Preferred Stock so as to make the rights or preferences of such series or class equal or senior to the Series A Preferred Stock.

- pay dividends on shares of the capital stock of the Company.

- effect any exchange or reclassification of any stock affecting the Series A Preferred Stock or any recapitalization involving the Company and its subsidiaries taken as a whole.

- repurchase or redeem, or agree to repurchase or redeem, any securities of the Company other than from employees of the Company upon termination of their employment pursuant to prior existing agreements approved by the Board of Directors of the Company.

- enter into any transaction with management or any member of the board of directors, except for employment contracts approved by the Board of Directors and transactions entered at arms-length terms which are no less favorable to the Company than could be obtained from unrelated third parties.

- effect any amendment of the Company's Certificate of Incorporation or Bylaws which would materially adversely affect the rights of the Series A Preferred Stock.

- incur or guarantee debt in excess of $100,000.

- voluntarily dissolve or liquidate.

- effect any merger or consolidation of the Company with or into another corporation or other entity (except one in the holders of the capital stock of the Company immediately prior to such a merger or consolidation continue to hold at least a majority of the capital stock of the surviving entity after the merger or consolidation) or sell, lease, or otherwise dispose of all or substantially all or a significant portion of the assets of the Company.

- Change the size of the Board of Directors or change any procedure of the Company relating to the designation, nomination, or election of the Board of Directors.

- Amend, alter, or repeal the preferences, special rights, or other powers of the Series A Preferred Stock so as to adversely affect the Series A Preferred Stock.

- Make capital expenditures of more than $25,000 in a single expenditure or an aggregate of $50,000 in any twelve-month period.

Liquidation Preference: The holders of Series A Preferred Stock shall have preference upon liquidation over all holders of Common Stock and over the holders of any other class or series of stock that is junior to the Series A Preferred Stock for an amount equal to the greater of (i) 3 times the amount paid for such Series A Preferred Stock and (ii) the amount which such holder would have received if such holder's shares of Series A Preferred Stock were converted to Common Stock immediately prior to such liquidation. Thereafter, the holders of Common Stock will be entitled to receive the remaining assets. For purposes of this section, a merger, consolidation, sale of all or substantially all of the Company's assets, or other corporate reorganization shall constitute a liquidation, unless the holders of at least a majority of the Series A Preferred Stock vote otherwise.

Board of Directors: The Board of Directors of the Company shall be composed of X members.

Options and Vesting TERMS TO BE DISCUSSED AS APPROPRIATE

Registration Rights: TERMS TO BE DISCUSSED AS APPROPRIATE

Affirmative Covenants: While any Series A Preferred Stock is outstanding, the company will:

- maintain adequate property and business insurance.

- comply with all laws, rules, and regulations.

- preserve, protect, and maintain its corporate existence; its rights, franchises, and privileges; and all properties necessary or useful to the proper conduct of its business.

- submit all reports required under Section 1202(d)(1)(C) of the Internal Revenue Code and the regulations promulgated thereunder.

- cause all key employees to execute and deliver noncompetition, nonsolicitation, nonhire, nondisclosure, and assignment of inventions agreements for a term of their employment with the Company plus one year in a form reasonably acceptable to the Board of Directors.

- do not enter into related party transactions without the consent of a majority of disinterested directors.

Financial Statements and Reporting: The Company will provide all information and materials, including, without limitation, all internal management documents, reports of operations, reports of adverse developments, copies of any management letters, communications with shareholders or directors, and press releases and registration statements, as well as access to all senior managers as requested by holders of Series A Preferred Stock. In addition, the Company will provide the holders of Series A Preferred Stock with unaudited monthly and quarterly and audited yearly financial statements, as well as an annual budget.

Redemption: Series A Preferred shareholders shall be redeemable upon demand by Series A shareholders equal to the following amounts (including accrued and unpaid dividends) at the indicated dates.

2 times original purchase price after 3 years
3 times original purchase price after 5 years

Right of First Refusal: Holders of Series A Preferred Stock shall have a pro rata right, based on their percentage of fully diluted equity interest in the company, with an undersubscription right up to the total number of shares being offered, to participate in subsequent stock issuances.

Right of First Refusal and Cosale: In the event that any of the Founders and existing executive management propose to sell their stock to third parties, the Company shall have the first right to purchase the securities on substantially the same terms as the proposed sale; the Series A Preferred Stockholders shall next have said right according to respective percentage ownership of Series A Preferred Stock or to sell proportionate percentage pursuant to cosale rights. Such rights shall terminate upon a Qualified Public Offering.

Other Provisions: The purchase agreement shall include standard and customary representations and warranties of the Company, and the other agreements prepared to implement this financing shall contain other standard and customary provisions. Definitive agreements will be drafted by counsel to the Investors. This term sheet is intended by the parties to be nonbinding.

Expenses: The Company will reimburse the holders of Series A Preferred Stock for reasonable legal fees in connection with the transaction, payable at closing and only in the event that the transactions contemplated by this term sheet are consummated, up to a limit of $5,000.

Additional Resources

Sample Term Sheet: http://www.drosenassoc.com/Draft%20Term%20 Sheet%20for%20Alliance%20of%20Angels.pdf

Model Term Sheet for Angel Investors: http://www. angelcapitaleducation.org/newsletter-detail/289-year.2010_289- id.209715290.html

Writing and Negotiating Term Sheets with a View toward Success: http://commonangels.wordpress.com/2008/03/28/term-sheets-2

* notes *

notes

* notes *

* notes *